APPLE-A-DAY

NUTRITIONAL REFERENCE AND COOKBOOK
FOR CHILDREN'S HEALTH AND WELLBEING

DOROTHY EDGELOW

The Children's Whole Health Foundation

MICHELLE ANDERSON PUBLISHING
Melbourne

First published in Australia 2006 by
Michelle Anderson Publishing Pty Ltd
P O Box 6032
Chapel Street North
South Yarra 3141
Tel: 03 9826 9028
Fax: 03 9826 8552
Email: mapubl@bigpond.net.au
Website: www.michelleandersonpublishing.com

Designed and typeset by: Norman Hurrell - Media Arts Communication
Cover photograph: Michael Johnson - Children at the Royal Botanic Gardens, Melbourne
Printed by: Griffin Press, Adelaide
Body systems diagrams: Paul Miller
National Library of Australia Cataloguing-in-Publication data

Edgelow, Dorothy
Apple a day : nutritional reference and cook book

ISBN 0 85572 366 1.

Cookery (Natural foods). 2. Children – Diseases – Diet
Therapy – Recipes. I. Children's Whole Health Foundation.
II. Title

641.563

Although every effort was made to provide current reliable information based on scientific data, the author and publishers accept no liability for any errors or omissions which may be present in this book, and no liability is accepted arising directly or indirectly as a result of reading or other use of this book. If the reader has any doubts about the recommendations made here, medical or other appropriate health consultation is advised.

Dedication

In recognition of all parents and child carers who bravely accept
the responsibility of raising children.

To the caring hearts of many wonderful people who helped put this book together
and to my husband Ken and our beautiful daughters
Lynette, Anne and Kerry and their families, who have given us
the most precious things in this life.

With love and deep gratitude, I thank you all.

Dorothy Edgelow

AN APPLE A DAY
KEEPS THE DOCTOR AWAY

BECAUSE......

APPLES ARE AN EXCELLENT SOURCE OF FIBRE, CARBOHYDRATES
AND PECTIN, WHICH PRODUCES A GEL (MALIC ACID) THAT HELPS TO KEEP
INTESTINES AND BOWELS CLEAN AND HEALTHY.

This well known adage has been used as a title
because the information offered is about prevention, which in turn
will hopefully eliminate a need for cure.

"WE MEET PEOPLE WHO GO TO EXTREMES IN DIET
AND WE FIND THAT THE BODY IS NOT AN EXTREME BUILDING.
IT IS A TEMPLE OF ALL THE DUST OF THE EARTH.
IT IS A TEMPLE OF ALL THE LOVING THINGS THAT YOU CAN PUT INTO IT,
AND YOU MUST TAKE LOVING CARE OF IT.
THIS IS THE TEMPLE OF THE LIVING SOUL.
WE FIND AS WE LOOK TO THIS TEMPLE, YOU HAVE ROOMS IN IT
JUST LIKE YOUR HOME.
YOU HAVE A LIVING ROOM. YES, YOU LIVE IN IT.
YOU HAVE A HOBBY ROOM WHERE YOU ENJOY.
YOU HAVE A BASEMENT WHERE YOU STORE THINGS.
YOU HAVE A FENCE AROUND YOUR HOUSE.
YOU HAVE A DRAUGHT SYSTEM, HEAT CIRCULATION.
BUT YOU HAVE STILL MORE.
YOU HAVE FURNITURE IN THAT HOME.
IT HAS DOORS THAT ARE OPEN TO ALLOW YOUR FRIENDS IN.
YOU HAVE THE WARMTH OF GOOD FEELING.
YES, IT IS ALL IN YOUR HOME, AND YOU ARE BUILT AS A HOME.
BUT REMEMBER, TOO, THAT WE HAVE TO FURNISH IT WITH LOVE.
YOU HAVE TO FURNISH IT WITH SOME OF THE LOVELIER THINGS IN LIFE,
LIKE PEACE AND JOY AND HAPPINESS."

Bernard Jensen Ph.D *Food Healing for Man*

CONTENTS

Acknowledgements

With heart felt thanks to the following people who have made this book possible.
The contribution of their knowledge and expertise offers a wide range of options to consider
when wanting to do the best you can for your child.

Sandy Harrison
BA, Grad Dip in Human Development
Grad Dip in Family Therapy

Roger Hersey
Management Consultant

Lance Shepherd
Grad Dip Psychology
Bachelor of Education,
Shiatsu Practitioner Level 4

Dr Angela Mackenzie
Royal Children's Hospital
FRACP, NB-BS

Dr Warwick Poon
Cert BS(Ins), Dip Ac, Cert OM, Cert HS
Cert PPT, Cert CHAACMA, AAII
Master of Paediatrics and Chinese Medicine

Ellen Rowatt
Registered Nurse Dip I
Grad Dip in Women's Health

Tim Maley
Valued supporter - Boulder, Colorado, USA

Louise Mahler
BE Com, B Music, Grad Dip Music
Master Applied SC

Suzie Quaife
ND, Dip Homeopathy
Member AHA, ATMS, AROH

Vicki Loughrey - Administration
Norman Hurrell - Publication Design
Paul Millar - Graphics
Jackie Jones - Editing
Michelle Anderson - Publisher

Introduction

What is the most precious gift you could possibly receive? If you search in your hearts, it will not be material things for they are all temporary. It will be something to do with love, that most fundamental and unique quality of the human kind, yet so carefully guarded and often hidden.

For me the most precious and treasured gift that has ever been offered is the trust of an innocent. The little hand sliding into mine saying, "I feel safe with you beside me in this big, wide and sometimes scary world." This is a mighty gift indeed and not given lightly but once given is a lifeline for a lifetime. To destroy this gift is to do untold and lasting damage.

For the developing child in today's society this is a fairly daunting world to contend with, even more so without the loving empathy of a caring adult to help guide them through the morass of 'growing up'. There are many 'lost' children battling through this storm, growing up in families that are preoccupied with the business of getting through yet another day. Socio-economics is no barrier to this dilemma. Children from all walks of life are experiencing a lack of appropriate guidance and effective role models in the formative years of their lives.

The reasons for this are a book in themselves and not what this book is about. It is instead about the way forward from now, not about finding blame in the past.

For that is a negative path and in truth most parents and care givers are doing the best they can with what they understand at this moment. I have a simple saying that I remind myself of often throughout the day 'Life is all about choice – choice in thought, action and feeling'. We are in total control of these and to think otherwise is to give our personal power away. The following pages are indeed about exercising your power of choice and to be a model of both 'right choice' and 'courage'. Courage to take responsibility for your own problems and in admitting to being a fallible human being and learning from our mistakes, a mistake after all just means more learning required.

In as much as this book is about helping your child it is also, upon reflection, about helping yourself. For we cannot truly be of any great and lasting support to another if we do not also have our own self in some order and understanding. So take the time to utilise the facilities, ideas and practices offered in this book and from The Children's Whole Health Foundation, with the view of helping your child to be the best person they can possibly be. Remember, that as a guide to your path, your choices are equally important for both of you. With a bit of luck and good honest work, who knows, you and your child may just begin to realise that that smile on the inside has always been there and that once found can never be taken away.

Lance Shepherd

Foreword

The creator of our world gave everything the ability to reproduce to ensure the continuity of all life. All parents should be able to know the joy of raising a happy, healthy child, but sometimes this gift comes along needing a manual on how, when and why and we think "what else can I do, except love, comfort, feed and house this child?". This book is my contribution, with information that I would like to have had when my children were small, so I am sitting here in my dressing gown trying to put the right words down on paper to inform and empower you, the loving parent.

I have worked in the food industry for more than 40 years. In 1978 at the age of 29 years, our eldest daughter Lynette was diagnosed with cancer and given a life expectancy of 6 to 12 months. With radiotherapy, a change in diet, some extra nutrition and positive thinking, she was well in less than six months and remains so.

Thinking diet was responsible for Lynette's condition, we opened four small restaurants, offering healthy food to the public and through a staff member, we met Dr Ian Gawler. I decided to help him with his vision of a Cancer Self Help Education Centre where for the last 21 years I have volunteered my knowledge of healthy food and lifestyle to the many thousands who come to the Centre. I recently wrote The Gawler Foundation Cookbook "A Recipe for Life".

Over the years, I have been asked by many how they can help their children to better health, which has prompted the idea of a range of "tools" that could be used to do this. I am no child expert, just a mother of three, grandmother of seven and great grandmother of two and a half so far, with a desire to help.

The emotional distress of children can go unnoticed in our busy life. They can appear to be okay with a situation but often a wrong pattern of thought is left in their mind. This pattern can affect their decisions and choices through life. Sometimes just a few moments of quiet discussion and a cuddle can have a huge effect. If you can allow time to address stressful situations at the time of happening it could prevent larger problems later in life. God's gift of children and the joy they bring is too precious to treat carelessly or to neglect. The quality of the child's life is dependent upon their parent or carer, we bring them into this world and they are our responsibility, not the school's, their friend's and certainly not the government's, they are ours.

It can be very helpful, in trying to determine what to do, when a child voices a preference for a certain food at a certain time. This food preference can be a clue to the nutritional needs of the little body. In the following pages there is information that can help you make an educated guess about what your child needs to keep growing and functioning well.

A nutritionally balanced diet is an important aspect of ensuring your child is off to a physically and emotionally healthy start in life. The appropriate food can, along with loving care and a little knowledge of the human system, make the raising of a child the joy it is meant to be and I know there is no other bond to match that of a parent and child. It is a true privilege to lovingly teach them life values and to help them understand the wonder of nature and human life.

This information was put together in the hope that it may encourage parents and child carers to seek out all the ways of nurturing their child and for them to feel empowered to make appropriate decisions based on their own knowledge (using medical advice if needed).

I also hope that it raises awareness of their child's physical and emotional needs; we are not just physical bodies, we have many levels that create our existence. To know and use all these levels to enhance our physical life can make a huge difference to our wellbeing.

You really are what you think, eat and aspire to. Being responsible for ourselves is the ultimate challenge.

The processing of much of our food today leaves it with very little nutritional value. The addition of over 50,000 chemical nutrients and additives is generally out of balance and is, as such, really not accepted as being beneficial by the body. Nature gives us food in balance, while the processing and marketing of that food can destroy it.

Too much processing and too many additives can spoil even organically grown food. Certainly, you do not have to deal with any added chemicals, but the food can be left with just basic fibre.

The allergies many suffer can be the result of chemicals and pesticides used to grow and process our food, including the chemical additives in wheat, sugar, milk, meat etc. These chemicals can be the cause of problems rather than the actual food in its unadulterated form.

The human body has twelve systems that work together to carry out the living process. Each of these systems has a specific function that works together to maintain balance in the body. If one system is not functioning well it affects the action of another, with energy (nutrition) stolen from another to maintain that action. Without proper nutrition supplying nutrients and, importantly, energy, a body can break down visibly in one area but with the problem needing to be addressed in a totally different system. This is because of the relationship between body systems. The Chinese concept of energy and food, discussed later in the book, explains this more fully.

The 12 body systems drawings used in this book are intentionally simplified, but were produced by a very talented graphic artist to illustrate and better help both you and your child understand the physical body and its workings.

Looking at a body's function from this perspective we need to be aware of the connectivity of these systems, how to keep them all healthy and where to look to remedy a problem. There is at times a need to use a medical solution for an urgent problem and this can be life-saving, but usually a long-term solution can be discovered with the use of any or many of the naturally based philosophies and modalities that are available to us today.

There are many factors other than physical ones that can affect human wellbeing and these factors can cause illness; by using natural therapies we can find the cause and hopefully eradicate it.

On a physical level we can understand the principle of nutrition and energy exchange and accept that if we eat correctly (digestive system) we will receive the necessary nutrients. These nutrients will be carried through the blood (circulatory system) to all the necessary areas via the glands (endocrine system), with their residue finally eliminated (excretory system).

There is also the approach of what is called mind-body medicine. This sounds very complicated but is really very simple. First of all we need to learn the marvellous physical mechanics of our body, then learn how to feed those functions and further enhance them by using visualisation and positive thoughts.

What we think about while eating and digesting our food can have a very big effect on what that food does for us. The best, most nutritious food can and may turn into a useless concoction if we are in a 'bad' state of mind. If we are angry, preoccupied, anxious, depressed or even over-excited, our system is compromised and can't do a good job.

Food is a blessing; it is the one thing we cannot live without and yet we treat it very casually. If we applied the same amount of time and energy to our food and nutrition as we do to many of our other physical needs, we would be much healthier and happier people.

There are many aspects and levels of health. Physical health can be achieved only when all the other functions of our body are in a healthy state. One of the most obvious areas that needs to be looked at is what I call "emotional nutrition". For a child this can only come from a secure, safe and happy home life. They need to be able to depend on their parents or carer in any circumstance, not just when they are being "good". Children in particular show a range of emotions for no obvious reason. Sometimes, taking the time to find out the cause before reacting can make a huge difference in the security that a child feels. Trust in a parent or carer can solve many difficult situations for a child and pave the way for a happy future.

When a child is afraid for any reason, he or she can seek attention in the wrong way, anything to gain that attention.

Behaving badly is a sure way to get someone's attention, which is better in their minds than no attention.

Children can also gain attention by not eating or by eating too much. Parents often give food as a panacea, which in later life accounts for many aspects of bad health including being overweight.

Much time and effort by many people produces the food that is available to us. Fresh unadulterated grains, vegetables and fruit can keep us fairly healthy but our thoughts, feelings and our physical environment play a part in how much we benefit from that food.

When preparing food for a meal as when getting ourselves a snack, try to look a the occupation as a joyful one. Food is a joy, it keeps us all, we can't live very long without it. We can go without water but we can't exist without food. You have worked hard for the money to buy food or worked hard to grow it. Food deserves respect. How you view what you are eating plays a part in what your body does with food. If you can visualise the nutrients being assimilated and taken to all parts of your body or your child's body, they can do this too; just show them the body organ sketches. Presenting well thought out foods to your child or family is a measure of your caring and love for them. Food is an opportunity to make a choice, make a good one and reap the rewards of a happy, well balanced child.

Meditation and a physical exercise like yoga are also important practices to incorporate into the lives of yourself and your children. One of the most beneficial forms of exercise a small child can enjoy doing is yoga. Yoga stimulates our endocrine system (refer to body systems diagram page 53) to perform more effectively. Skipping, running, stretching all encourage balance of growth.

Deep breathing, consciously practised for only a few minutes can really boost the immune system and keep the respiratory system clear. Singing loudly or chanting affirmations made up to sing to a tune the child recognises can help both you and your child's lungs to take in oxygen needed by the blood. Expressions of joy and happiness, even small ones have an affect on our organs. Different emotions affect different organs; joy and happiness open all channels of energy to work effectively. Worry, negative thoughts, anger and blame all close up, tighten and restrict that energy exchange, leading to a malnourished cell that can't do its job properly.

The human body is not a bunch of atoms fused together, we are not a man made mechanical object that operates automatically, although it may appear that we do.
Our unique spirit that operates from a base of love controls the functions that keep us alive and healthy, or sometimes not so healthy, depending on our emotions, our thoughts and actions.

We can sabotage ourselves and our children very easily, by not showing our love, not caring how we relate to each other, being too busy and pre-occupied with material needs.
We have the opportunity to show a good example of how to live happily to our children. They in turn will not need to depend on advertised products and activities to make them feel secure.

Food that does not contribute to health, sweet, fried and processed are devoid of nutrients. Overeating in order to find comfort and satisfaction are dangerous situations for your child's future health.

Given emotional nutrition they will feel safe and secure, behave well, concentrate on activities when needed, relate well to each other and to their parents and above all be happy. The early childhood experiences of life lay the foundation of how they will function as an adult. Their sense of values should be given by the parent.

The human experience is to understand and find love, practice unconditional love and we as parents can help them to experience that. Don't waste the opportunity and regret it later.

Take time to get to know your child, showing that child in many ways that you love them. Respecting them and considering the outcome of your actions or non-actions in the very early years will supply that "emotional nutrition", they will then have the most valuable nutrition.

I have asked some very experienced people who deal with children to offer some information that could be helpful in bringing up your child. There are many ways of promoting health and I really appreciate their contribution.

Dorothy Edgelow

HAND IN HAND

WALKING WITH MY CHILD ALONG LIFE'S PATH –
A BOND LIKE NO OTHER CAN BE.

A CLOSENESS IN FLESH AND SPIRIT-
FAR MORE THAN WE CAN SEE.

FROM SHARING A BODY TO WALKING ALONE-
SO CLOSE, YET WE ARE FREE.

HAND IN HAND , WE WALK ALONG LIFE'S PATH-
TOGETHER IN ETERNITY.

S Harrison

Reflections

"AND A WOMAN WHO HELD A BABY AGAINST HER BOSOM SAID,

SPEAK TO US OF CHILDREN.

AND HE SAID:

YOUR CHILDREN ARE NOT YOUR CHILDREN.

THEY ARE THE SONS AND DAUGHTERS OF LIFE'S LONGING FOR ITSELF.

THEY COME THROUGH YOU BUT NOT FROM YOU,

AND THOUGH THEY ARE WITH YOU YET THEY BELONG NOT TO YOU.

YOU MAY GIVE THEM YOUR LOVE BUT NOT YOUR THOUGHTS,

FOR THEY HAVE THEIR OWN THOUGHTS.

YOU MAY HOUSE THEIR BODIES BUT NOT THEIR SOULS,

THEIR SOULS DWELL IN THE HOUSE OF TOMORROW,

WHICH YOU CANNOT VISIT, NOT EVEN IN YOUR DREAMS.

YOU MAY STRIVE TO BE LIKE THEM,

BUT SEEK NOT TO MAKE THEM LIKE YOU.

FOR LIFE GOES NOT BACKWARD NOT TARRIES WITH YESTERDAY.

YOU ARE THE BOWS FROM WHICH YOUR CHILDREN AS LIVING

ARROWS ARE SENT FORTH."

Kahlil Gibran *The Prophet*

6

Feeding Your Newborn

There are many ways of feeding your baby if is not your choice, and there are many valid reasons for choosing alternative ways of nourishing your baby. If breast feeding is stressful for any reason it is better for other options to be utilized; the emotional and physical health of both mother and child need to be carefully considered. If you decide to bottle feed your baby, there are choices other than the regular baby food formulas.

Choices of milk

In most cases, mother's milk is, of course, ideal as it provides baby with four times the linoleic acid of other milks and this acid is needed to encourage brain and the nervous system development. Baby's immune system is also activated by bacillus bifidus (beta lactose) from mother's milk.

Cow's milk has been shown to be deficient in some vitamins, and minerals are not present in the same ratio as in human milk. In addition, the type of lactose in cow's milk, called alpha lactose, doesn't produce the necessary flora in a baby's intestines.

Goat's milk can be a good choice. It has similar nutritional properties to cow's milk but as goats are generally not fed a large amount of grass or other food contaminated with pesticides and chemicals, the milk is of a better quality. Goat's milk has a softer curd and smaller fat globules than cow's milk, making it homogenized in its natural state and easier to digest for young and old.

Soy milk is a good source of calcium and protein and the necessary fatty acid, alpha linoleic acid. Although used as a substitute for mother's or cow's milk, consultation should be made with the relevant specialist if you decide you would like to use soy milk as a primary milk for a young baby. Nevertheless, incorporating soy milk with other food and drinks can be very beneficial, as there is good nutrition in soy beans and their by-products.

Soy has twice the iron content of cheese, meat and eggs and three times more phosphorus than chicken. (Phosphorus is essential for the nervous system). Soy is also an alkalizing food; sore throats and reflux condition can be caused by an over-acid stomach.

Oat, almond and rice milks (recipes later in the book) are also useful at times, adding nutrients that are not available from other foods.

Solid foods

When baby is ready for solid foods it is better for digestion that solid food be given at a different time to milk. Milk, like fruit, digests better when given on its own. As well as providing the comfort of good digestion, the nutrient content of milk and fruit is better assimilated when taken on its own.

Choosing to raise your child on a vegetarian diet always raises the question of adequate nutrition, especially protein. Over many years of study and application, a healthy vegetarian diet has been proven possible where there is a well-balanced diet of grains, vegetables and fruit and their by-products, and extra protein from sea vegetables and soured dairy products if required. The omega 3s in fish oil are useful for supplying extra nutrients, as is cold-extracted flaxseed oil.

A suggested ratio of foods during and after weaning are:

· 40%-60% grains and cereals – oats, rice, millet
· 20%-40% vegetables, green leafy are the best
· 5%-10% legumes beans, chick peas and dairy if liked (plain yoghurt and add your own fruit)
· 5%-10% fruit – eg. apples and bananas are better to start with and you can add a small amount of ground nuts, seeds and sea vegetables.

When starting your baby on solid food consider using non gluten grains and organic vegetables. Using these can provide a good balance of the acid-alkaline levels in the baby's body and, by restricting the acid forming foods, you allow better digestion and absorption. Baby's first introduction to cereal is best done with brown rice, either cooked by you or bought as ready-prepared cereal. Rice is more easily digested than wheat and some of the prepared cereals are predominantly wheat. There could be a problem with wheat as it is very acidic to the body and as babies often have a reaction to the introduction of new foods, care should be taken particularly if they are acidic.

Pureed vegetables are the next best step in introducing new foods after cereals; try them singly at first and then a few mixtures. You can also add a little creamed cheese occasionally. Fairly thick soups with some wholemeal toast can be a useful way of feeding baby and yourself at lunchtimes.

Some acid forming foods are wheat, rye, barley and, to a lesser extent, oats, cow's milk, sugars and the over use of protein foods. Some alkaline forming foods are vegetables, rice, millet and tree-ripened fruits.

Fruit juices aren't always all that they seem: commercial juices contain a high percentage of sugar and not much else. Even freshly juiced fruit can also contain a lot of sugar. Vegetable juices are a better choice, as they are cleansing and rebuild the cells and blood.

FORTUNATE PEOPLE
ARE THOSE WHO BELIEVE THEY ARE.

PLACE INSIDE

THERE IS A LITTLE PLACE INSIDE MYSELF
WHERE WISDOM REIGNS
IN ADDITION "KNOWING" JUST IS.

WHERE ALL THE ANSWERS I HAD BEEN
SEEKING ARE THERE,
CLEAR AS DAY,
TO GUIDE THE WAY FORWARD,
IN STRENGTH AND TRUTH.

CALL IT THE LITTLE VOICE OF INTUITION,
A MOTHERS/FATHERS "KNOWING",
WHISPERS FROM THE SOUL-
WHO KNOWS?

BUT THERE IS A PLACE INSIDE MYSELF-
WHERE I KNOW,
AS ONLY A PARENT CAN KNOW,
WHAT IS BEST FOR MY CHILD.

MAY I REST THERE OFTEN.
MAY I HEAR THE WHISPERS CLEARLY.
MAY I TRUST AND FOLLOW...SH...

Feeding Your Toddler

Breakfast

1) A breakfast of cooked cereal is recommended, preferably oats as they do not cause the problems that wheat can. You can also add some ground nuts and seeds and some grain malts instead of sugar or honey. Try to avoid processed cereals as they usually contain lots of sugar, unbalanced mineral and vitamin additions and the processing leaves them empty of vital nutrients.

2) Wholegrain bread is a second choice with an appropriate spread.

3) Fresh fruit with natural yoghurt and a milk-based drink.
This is a third choice.

Snack Foods are suggested in the recipe section (page 130).

Lunch

A lunch of cooked or raw vegetables or egg is recommended, and you can add some well-cooked legumes at times or sandwiches with nutritious fillings, not just margarine and jam. Sandwich fillings are suggested below.

Fresh or dried fruit is good for a mid-afternoon snack .

Main Meal

For the main meal, provide thick pureed soups that include grains or a non-gluten grain such as rice, some starch vegetables and plenty of green leafy vegetables. There should be a minimum of pasta (as it is highly processed) and a small quantity of fish (or chicken or meat for those who want it). Occasionally, you can mash some egg into the vegetables.

Small children can gain a lot of nutrients from sea vegetables (kombu and nori) chopped small or crushed. These vegetables may seem a little strange to some, but are extremely high in all nutrients (refer to nutrient charts pages 36-41).

Sandwich Fillings

· Almond or hazelnut butter with slices of apple and jam on top of slice.
· Mashed banana, chopped nuts or nut spread with drizzled honey.
· Mashed banana on toasted raisin bread.
· Tomato, mayonnaise, sprouts and chopped spinach.
· Split pitta bread filled with chopped left-over chicken or beef mixed with mayonnaise, adding lettuce and bean sprouts.
· Salad vegetables rolled up on sorj bread.
· Pitta bread filled with cream cheese, grated carrot and crushed pineapple.
· Pitta or Lebanese bread filled with any meat and potato salad.
· Flaked tuna with cucumber, mayonnaise and lettuce.
· Add sprouts to a sandwich for a vitamin boost.

NO COMMUNICATION
LEADS TO CONFUSION,
WHICH LEADS TO CONFLICT

AN ACORN
IS AS PERFECT AS A
FULLY GROWN OAK TREE

Feeding Your Primary School Child

There is much evidence to support the importance of children having a nourishing breakfast. They will be calmer and can concentrate better and therefore be a lot happier.

- Your primary school child could have cooked cereal or wholegrain toast and egg or some cheese or animal products, yoghurt and fruit.
- Commercial fruit yoghurts are not as beneficial as plain natural yoghurt with added fresh fruit.
- Milk drink or a smoothie. Recipes for smoothies are in the recipe sheets on page 134.
- A piece of hard fruit or vegetable sticks for morning tea is suggested by school dietitians.

Lunch is best in the form of nutritionally filled sandwiches. Suggestions are on page 130. A container of salad vegetables, yoghurt and fruit is also a good lunch. Don't provide too much as children prefer to play at this time.

When home after school try to avoid the pitfall of biscuits, sweets and sweet drinks and pasta. These foods can cause changes in behaviour: a big sugar boost over-activates your children's behaviour. Giving these foods at this time means that the unused and undigested sugar may cause an increase in weight. Sugar which is a simple carbohydrate (simple carbohydrate is a pure carbohydrate and lacks all the nutrients required for digestion), goes straight to the bloodstream with no added value and does not replace any essential nutrients. The balance of calcium and phosphorus is severely affected by sugar, both are almost destroyed. Sugar also lowers the immune system.

Diabetes and excessive weight gain could be avoided in many instances if refined, processed and chemically changed foods were not part of a young child's diet. These types of foods lack enzymes, the spark of life. We need plant life as close to natural as possible to survive. All good food starts from plants: animals eat plants, fish eat plants, and birds eat nuts and seeds.

Fast foods, all types sold to take-away or eat in are not as nutritious as they should be, regardless of how they are advertised. Food for this purpose is kept in storage for long periods then prepared, allowing oxidisation, and then kept in refrigeration for longer periods again. Vegetables and fruits lose their food value shortly after picking, and much of it is picked unripe anyway and so the nutrients are not fully developed. Fast foods also contain saturated fats and sugar substitutes, which are not healthy either. Once a child develops a taste for these foods, it is very hard to change the pattern. The best and easiest way to teach a child good eating habits, is by example. This is not easy in our society with so many multiples of choice with food.

Some childhood problems are genetic but a lot could be avoided by feeding the baby a good diet initially. For example, respiratory problems can stem from the incomplete processing and digestion of dairy foods and wheat.

Acid and alkaline is mentioned frequently in this book. The explanation of this reference is to help you and your family to be aware of as many ways as possible to be healthy. The presence of sugar fats and protein in so much of our general diet is one of the causes of our bodily pH being out of balance. Everything on the planet, including we humans, has a pH balance. Our food intake should be a ratio of 75%-80% alkaline-forming foods and 20%-25% of acid forming foods. Refer to the nutritional charts on pages 36-41.

We can also cause our bodies to be too acidic by our emotions, our environment, our way of life and our negative thoughts. All these play a part. We must have a body that is too acidic to be vulnerable to catching a cold.

Anxiety, tension and fear play a part in many problems as these emotions can cause restriction in nutrient pathways and organs resulting in the malfunction of, and energy loss to, many parts of the body. When you remember that even plants need a pH balance to grow well or to not grow at all, it's a little easier to grasp this concept.

Affirmations for Children

I AM A GOOD FRIEND TO MYSELF.

I PLAY WELL WITH OTHERS.

MY IMAGINATION IS FABULOUS.

I CAN DO ANYTHING I SET MY MIND TO.

I FEEL HAPPY.

I CAN BE WHATEVER I WANT TO BE.

I AM UNIQUE AND SPECIAL.

I AM HEALTHY AND STRONG.

I FEEL GREAT.

EVERY DAY IN EVERY WAY I AM GETTING BETTER AND BETTER.

I FEEL CALM AND RELAXED.

I AM TOTALLY HEALTHY.

I AM SAFE.

I'M DOING THE BEST I CAN.

I LOVE MYSELF.

TODAY IS A WONDERFUL DAY.

IT IS SAFE FOR ME TO GROW UP.

11

NUTRIENTS

Proteins

Proteins are components of all cells. They stick everything together and are necessary for the growth of all internal organs and for the quality of the muscles, blood, hair and nails. They are made up of amino acids and animal foods generally contain all 16 amino acids, called Complete Proteins.

One plant food will not contain all the necessary amino acids, but if we have a good mix of vegetables and grains we obtain all the essential amino acids. We only need small amounts (25 grams) of animal foods to supply enough protein for body repair and building. The other 40% protein suggested as a daily requirement is used for other purposes by our body. Too much results in many conditions that lead to illness. Proteins in all forms are acid to our system and in excess can cause excessive weight gain, dehydration, cancer and many other problems. The residue of meat fibre left after basic digestion is a major cause of bowel problems as our bowel is very long and meat fibre putrefies very quickly, getting stuck along the way. Fish, grains and legumes are a better choice of protein. Sea vegetables are also good sources of protein and have the advantage of being processed in the system without side effects. Dairy (milk and cheese) contribute to mucus and are not handled too well by many, particularly children.

Protein Foods

- Fresh nuts (but not peanuts as they contain aflotoxins which are a carcinogenic fungus resulting from the chemical spraying of the soils, essential for growing peanuts).
- All sea vegetables – nori, arame, hijiki, kelp, kombu, agar agar.
- Fish – preferably deep sea fish.
- Soy products – tofu, tempeh, yoghurt, milk

- Lentils
- Chick peas
- Lima and Kidney beans
- Barley
- Alfalfa
- Meat, chicken
- Corn
- Dairy – milk, cheese, yoghurt, keffir
- Bread – small amount in some breads.

Vegetables and fruits have a minimal protein content but are an essential part of a balanced diet. Often, parents are concerned that providing a vegetarian diet means they are not supplying enough protein, but if you check the charts (page 36-41) you will see that protein is easy to obtain.

Protein required:
Adult: 58-70 grams daily
Child (3-7 yrs):   26-50 grams daily
Infant (1 yr):   3   grams daily

Carbohydrates

Carbohydrates come in two forms: complex and simple.

Complex Carbohydrates

Our bodies function better when most of our carbohydrate intake is in the form of what are called complex carbohydrates, which are found in grains, legumes, seeds, nuts, vegetables and fruit. The components of carbohydrates are starch, sugar and cellulose (or fibre). During digestion, the carbohydrates from these foods are broken down and transformed into glucose. Some of this 'blood' sugar is used as fuel for the brain tissue, nervous system and muscles. This type of carbohydrate also regulates protein and fat metabolism. The starches in carbohydrate foods are assimilated slowly to help keep the glucose level in the blood constant. Fibre is essential for correct functioning of the bowel and elimination processes.

Carbohydrates are needed for energy but can be converted to fat by the body. Complex carbohydrates can be burned by the body to produce energy.

Protein is also needed and used by the body for energy and if the right kind of carbohydrates are ingested the protein is free of the job of producing energy and can concentrate on other needs.

Carbohydrates can be a problem if too many are eaten, particularly in the form of pasta. Carbohydrates give a quick boost of energy because they are converted to a type of sugar. Most pastas are so highly refined and processed that there is no nutrient of lasting value left in the product.

Simple Carbohydrates

Simple carbohydrates (plain sugar) give a short energy boost and then deplete the body of other nutrients. They are found in all baked goods such as cakes, buns and biscuits, and sweetened foods, drinks and confectionery.

If you are concerned about your weight it is useful to know that, according to some medical studies, the digestion of carbohydrates slows down after 4.00 p.m. Food that is not properly digested can be stored as fat by the body.

Calcium

Calcium is a very necessary mineral needed by almost all parts of the body to function. If a child is allergic to dairy, calcium can be obtained from other sources and can be 'manufactured' or increased by the body if some vitamin D (sunshine) is available to the child. Calcium can also be supplied by some of the green leafy vegetables, sprouted seeds or grains and sea vegetables. For a young child, of course, these foods need to be prepared appropriately. Vegetables need to be pureed or mashed very well, seeds ground, and sea vegetables (the highest source of calcium on the planet) soaked and then chopped small

and mixed in with other foods. Only minute amounts of sea vegetable are needed.

Unless food is able to be chewed well (to incorporate the saliva), the nutrients in any food will not be completely assimilated. In a small child this cannot happen properly, so the food needs to be broken down as much as possible so that the child can move it around in its mouth, mixing in some saliva. As dairy is acidic to the body and can contribute to pH imbalance, many children and some adults develop a condition called lactose intolerance from the use of cow's milk and its by-products. In the past, the whole untreated milk did not cause as many problems as the highly processed milk and milk products of today do. These modern products are out of balance, can be difficult to digest with their extra additives, and the fats needed for assimilation are taken out. The many processes that are used to give milk a longer shelf life do not allow the product to be as beneficial as it could be in its natural state. Natural yoghurt from any milk is usually assimilated well, and you can add your own fruit when needed. Children who can't tolerate milk can usually handle soured or fermented milk products. If you can give your baby a few drops of flaxseed oil daily, you will greatly increase their ability to be healthy. Soy, oat, rice and almond milk are all sources of calcium (although no one should be used exclusively by children as they are not a complete food). These milks can be made at home if they are preferred to commercial varieties.

Vegetables and grains also contain calcium. Exercise in all forms helps the body to develop even more calcium. Sea vegetables (seaweeds) are becoming more familiar to those in western society and contain very large amounts of almost all the nutrients that humans need. Seaweeds are an excellent source of calcium and minerals as well as protein and iodine, which we need in small amounts to balance our thyroid action.

Vitamins

Vitamins are not able to be produced by our bodies and so have to be ingested from a well balanced diet. There are thirteen essential vitamins and others that are only needed in minute amounts.

Fat soluble vitamins A, D, E, & K can be stored by the body to be used as needed.

Water soluble vitamins B5, C, Biotin, Folic acid and Pantothenic acid cannot be stored and need constant renewal as any excess is excreted through urine and perspiration

Deficiencies could lead to:

Vitamin A –
Bronchial infection and problems in the respiratory tract
Blurred vision and other eye problems
Difficulty digesting fats
Rickets (softening of the bones)

Vitamin B1 –
(Thiamine)
Depression, confusion, poor appetite
Crohns Disease, Ulcerative Colitis
Swelling of the ankles and feet
Inability to concentrate

Vitamin B2 -
(Riboflavin)
Mouth ulcers, scaling around the nose, ears, mouth and forehead
Intolerance to bright light
Inflammations, inability to urinate
Lack of concentration, depression

Vitamin B3 -
(Niacin)
Headaches and general tiredness
Arthritis, arteriosclerosis,
General irritation of digestive mucus membranes

Vitamin B5 -
(Pantothenic Acid)
Adrenal and muscular exhaustion
Low blood sugar
Decrease in antibody formation
Muscular cramps

Vitamin B6 -
(Pyridoxine)
Fluid retention, cramps, constipation
Anaemia, convulsions, migraine
Parkinson's Disease

Vitamin B12 -
Mental slowness and disturbances, pernicious anaemia, herpes
Glandular fever, anorexia, unpleasant body odor

Folic Acid -
Leukemia, anaemia, arteriosclerosis
Mental and physical tiredness

14

Choline -   High cholesterol levels
High blood pressure, loss of hair
Heart palpitations, visual disturbances, liver and kidney problems

Vitamin D -   Rickets in children, poor metabolism
Tetany (muscular membrane flabbiness)

Vitamin E -   Problems with the reproductive and circulatory systems
Reduction of oxygen and nutrient transportation in the body

Minerals

There are at least fifteen minerals needed in minute amounts for health. Sometimes, when a diet is low in good quality fruit, vegetables and grains, supplements are needed but advice should be sought from a qualified practitioner.

Calcium	Iodine	Potassium
Chlorine	Iron	Silica
Chlorophyll	Manganese	Sodium
Copper	Magnesium	Sulphur
Fluorine	Phosphorous	Zinc

NEVER EAT WHEN YOU FEEL SICK, TIRED, ANGRY OR UPSET.

LET YOUR SPIRIT SHINE

AND CHOOSE A HEALTHY PATTERN OF LIVING —

IT IS YOUR CHOICE.

LIVE VITAL FOODS, CREATE LIVE VITAL CELLS,

WHICH ARE NECESSARY

FOR VITAL LIVING.

Dairy Products

Butter

Although butter is a saturated fat it is a better choice for a spread than the chemically produced margarine. Butter goes through three almost natural processes to be made. Clarified butter (ghee) is actually of benefit to our system because the process of clarifying produces butyric acid, a mono-unsaturated oil that protects the heart. To make a quite healthy spread, mix softened butter with half the volume of olive oil (2:1) and refrigerate. To keep it firm at room temperature add the same quantity of lecithin granules as oil to the mixture (2:1:1).

Cheese

Cheese in all forms is a saturated fat and best used sparingly. The cheese making process makes it harder for our system to access the nutrients that are available from whole unadulterated milk.

Seed Cheese

Seed cheese is high in vitamins and enzymes and is easy to make and digest. You can add herbs, onion, garlic and any savoury seasoning you like. It is great spread on crackers or when used to stuff small tomatoes, mushrooms etc.

You will need ½ cup sunflower seeds, or almonds or cashews, and 1 cup of filtered water.

Method

Put the seeds or nuts in a glass jar, cover with filtered water and let them soak overnight. Drain and rinse. Place seeds and 1 cup of filtered water in a blender and run blender until mixture is creamy. Return mixture to the jar and let it sit in a warm place or in a pan of hot water for 5-9 hours or until it separates (into curds and whey). Take the soft cheese part off the top and refrigerate or place the mixture in a cheesecloth and squeeze tightly, letting this "bag" hang over a bowl for a day, making for a firmer cheese.

(For Milk see page 25)

Meat

The reason meat is suggested as a possible source of nutrients (for protein and some vitamins) is because these nutrients are more easily assimilated than those same nutrients obtained from the vegetable kingdom.

- Only a small quantity is required to satisfy the need some people feel for meat .
- The main part of a meal should be vegetable and grain.

If possible, buy your meat and dairy from an organic/bio-dynamic source, as a lot of the chemicals fed to most animals become concentrated in their fat, and regular over-consumption of these chemicals can result in the forming of mucus, urea and uric acid (gout).

We, as humans, have a very long intestinal tract and there are many processes food must go through before we eliminate the residue we don't need. Often, this residue takes a long time to pass through our system and fibre can get 'stuck' on the way, leaving an opportunity for unhealthy bacteria to develop in our bowel which can lead to disease. The fat in and on meat is also saturated fat and cannot be processed through our system with ease. Food transit time through our system should be in the 18-24 hours bracket.

Beef

Lean beef can provide many essential nutrients, particularly B12 & iron. A 100 gram serving once each week is sufficient to provide the needed B12 and iron for most adults. For children, 25-50 grams of lean beef each week is sufficient.

Chicken

Unless organic free range chickens can be obtained they cannot be chosen as a good food, particularly for children. The chicken industry uses many chemicals to improve the growing time for chickens. A chicken can be brought to adult size in 45 days from hatching. Steroids, hormones and antibiotics are used in huge amounts to produce fat chickens fast and these chemicals remain in the meat. A good, free range organic chicken can contain protein, phosphorous, potassium and chlorine.

Pork

Pork meat must be cooked extremely well (no liquid running out when cut) to eliminate to a large extent the ferments, uric acid and xanthin, both of which are poisonous.

Fish

Fish is a better source of protein than meat. Fish also has the decided advantage of supplying omega 3, an essential fatty acid that, among many other uses, keeps the blood viscosity at a level where it doesn't form clots. Deep sea fish are the most beneficial as they supply a good quantity of cobalt, iodine and fluorine, as well as the omegas.
200-300 grams of fish each week is sufficient to supply the body's needs of these and many other nutrients.

Shellfish can be full of toxins and low in fatty acids, so keep them to a minimum.

Sweeteners

Sugar

Sugar is a major force in our bodies and we need it, but in the right form. The sugars in whole foods are balanced with the proper minerals and the energy obtained from the breaking down of these sugars is enduring. The highs and lows we experience from taking in refined sugars (hidden in so many processed foods) cause, among many other conditions, an acid effect in the body, an upset mineral balance, and lowering of the immune system. This leads to a blood sugar imbalance and more sugar cravings, as well as an increase in the craving for meat and other high protein foods. Grains and vegetables chewed very well will gradually reduce the cravings for sweetness from the wrong sources.

Honey

In small quantities, honey can be substituted for sugar, but honey is highly refined by bees and has more calories than white sugar. Raw cold extracted honey does contain some minerals and enzymes and does not upset the body's mineral balance.

Grain Malts

Made from fermented rice or barley, grain malts are only one-third as sweet as sugar yet contain complex sugars and many of the nutrients in grains. They take longer to digest so they don't produce the highs and lows that one can experience when eating cane sugar.

Stevia Powder or Liquid

Becoming better known, stevia is a small herb that is native to Latin America and the southern United States. The leaves and flowers of this plant are thirty times sweeter than sugar, and stevia can be used without ill effect by diabetics. Stevia does not work as well as other sweeteners in baked goods because

it doesn't have the moistening effect of cane sugar.

Fruit Concentrates

Fruit concentrates are another source of sweetening, but because of their concentrated nature, their sugar content becomes very high. Fruit concentrates are far from being whole unprocessed foods. Dried fruits which have been soaked well in water can be pureed and used as sweeteners.

Cane Sugar Substitutes

Not all recipes will work with sugar substitutes. One cup of white sugar is equivalent to:
- ¾ cup pure maple syrup reduce total liquids by 2 tablespoons
- ½ cup honey reduce total liquids by ¼ cup
- 1 cup molasses - reduce liquids by ½ cup
- 1½ cup sorghum reduce total liquids by ¼ cup
- 1 cup pure corn syrup reduce total liquids by ¼ cup
- 1 square of cooking chocolate is equivalent to 1 tablespoon of carob powder (when using carob powder use a little less sweetening than the recipe calls for as carob is a natural sweetener)
- when using substitutes, prevent burning by lowering the baking temperature by 20°C (40°F)
- to measure liquid sweeteners, first moisten cup with hot water
- use unsweetened fruit juice in place of other liquid
- fructose (fruit sugar) can be used to replace sugar in cereals, drinks and desserts (be careful that you are not allergic to the fruit from which the sugar is derived)
- when substituting glucose or dextrose for sugar, remember they are usually derived from corn
- in baking, use dried fruits to add sweetness.

Eggs

While eggs are classed as a good protein source with eight amino acids, they can also be one of the most common allergenic foods. They are best kept very cool and all products using eggs should be cooked thoroughly as salmonella can penetrate the porous egg shell and thus make uncooked eggs quite dangerous. Chickens enclosed in poultry farms are devoid of almost all nutrients. So check the labeling on egg containers as they can be misleading. Compare free-range eggs purchased from a health food shop with eggs produced commercially.

Eggs have a number of functions in baked products and it is not possible to replace all of these with substitutes. Eggs act as a structural component and nutrient source, providing lightness, flavour and moisture.
Structure is not severely affected by omitting eggs as long as a binder and sufficient liquid is added (3 tablespoons for every egg omitted).

The nutrient quality of eggs cannot be substituted and lecithin in egg yolk acts as an emulsifier for the fat in baked goods, helping to break down the fat particles.

In egg-free recipes the fat is often melted and boiled with the liquid and quickly stirred into the dry ingredients to stop dispersion of the fat and water. The lecithin in the egg yolk breaks up the fat, so for a 1 egg alternative substitute:
- 2 tablespoons cold cooked sago (only successful for substituting up to 2 eggs)
- 2 tablespoons flour, ½ teaspoon seasoning, ½ teaspoon baking powder and 2 tablespoons liquid
- 2 tablespoons water, ½ teaspoon baking powder (good in biscuit/cake recipes requiring only 1 egg)
- 1 mashed banana in biscuits, cakes, pancakes & muffins.

Also:
- gelatin works well in puddings and desserts: 1 tablespoon to every 2 cups liquid
- 250 grams dried apricots soaked in water for several hours or overnight. Blend, add extra water if necessary, strain and store in refrigerator: one generous tablespoon will substitute for 1 egg (freeze portions for further use).
- Ground flaxseed is a good egg substitute in biscuit, cake, pancake and muffin recipes. Add 1 cup ground flaxseed to 3 cups cold water. Bring to boil, stirring constantly. Boil for 3 minutes, cool and store in the refrigerator in a closed jar: 1 tablespoon will substitute for 1 egg.
- Replace egg as the binder in meat loaf or rissoles with 1 cup puffed rice to each 500 grams mince.
- Use tapioca or arrowroot flour as binders. Instead of using 2 cups rice flour, use 1½ cups flour and ½ cup tapioca/arrowroot plus 2 teaspoons extra liquid.

Carob

The carob tree is one of the oldest known fruit-bearing trees. It originated in the Mediterranean region and was known as St John's bread.

- Carob flour and powder supply protein, carbohydrates, minerals, calcium and phosphorous.
- Carob has a very low fat content.
- Carob can be used as a substitute for chocolate or coffee in cooked products and in hot or cold drinks .
- Carob needs no added sweeteners.
- Carob is an alkaline-forming food and does not contain caffeine.
- Carob chocolate usually contains coconut or palm oil fats (saturated fat).

Legumes

Beans, peas and lentils are an important source of protein and are good for the kidneys. They are often avoided because of problems with flatulence and allergies. These problems may be due to improper preparation and cooking or poor combinations (wrong choice of legume). Legumes such as great northern, navy, fava, lima, mung beans and chick peas (garbanzo) should be soaked in cold water overnight if possible.

Legumes are time-consuming but worth the trouble. Preparation and cooking can be a mystery, but once you get into the routine of using this very important food you will be amazed at the variety you can get in your meals.

Soaking promotes digestibility, faster cooking and makes more minerals available. It also starts the sprouting process and eliminates phytic acid. Always cook beans separately, then add to other dishes.

- Soak them overnight, with a strip of kombu (seaweed) in cold water.
- Cover them well with water because beans are very absorbent.
- Pour off soaking water when ready to cook (gas-producing enzymes are released into the soak water).
- Add fresh water, adding back the kombu and bring to the boil.
- Pour off this water, add more fresh water (and the kombu) and cook till tender – varies from ½ to 1 hour.
- Add 1 teaspoon cumin or fennel for each cup of beans, if desired.
- Add a little tamari, miso, cider vinegar or sea salt when beans are almost cooked, if desired.
- Rinse beans well and use hot or cold with many varieties of dressing, or added to soups/casseroles.

Lentils

Lentils do not require much preparation. It is generally not necessary to soak them, but this does improve their digestibility. If you decide not to soak them, wash well, removing all small stones or other foreign objects (often they have quite a lot). Cook in plenty of water, although they do not expand as much as legumes and only take about 20 to 30 minutes to cook. Lentils can be cooked with other foods in the same pot.

Sprouting Grains and Seeds

Grains and seeds are at their greatest stage of vitality when sprouted. They then have a dramatic increase in vitamin and enzyme content. Protein is turned into amino acids and crude fat is broken down into free fatty acids, making the nutrients easier to digest and assimilate. Most sprouts that come from large grains are better cooked lightly. You can sprout alfalfa, lentils, mung beans, sunflower, wheat and rye.
To sprout:
- soak 2 tablespoons of seeds for at least twelve hours in a wide-mouthed jar
- (covering mouth of jar with muslin or sprouting screen and secure with rubber band)
- drain and stand upright so excess water drains away
- rinse twice daily until sprouts are ready
- best eaten when there are two small leaves showing.

Alfalfa sprouts: this tiny plant, when grown in soil, can produce roots up to thirty metres long, thus reaching many minerals and nutrients not reached by other plants.

Alfalfa sprouts clean the intestines and take harmful acids out of the blood.
They contain ample protein, carotene (equal to carrots), calcium, iron and magnesium, which is why they are recommended in healthy diets.

Grains

Wheat, barley, rice, millet, buckwheat, oats and corn are all extremely important in a well balanced diet. When prepared properly, they satisfy hunger and taste good. They provide energy and endurance and when combined with legumes and vegetables, supply all the elements of nutrition necessary for human development. Grains must be chewed properly to incorporate saliva, which is needed to start the digestion process.

Soaking in cold water for several hours, or overnight if possible, helps to release the nutrients that make grains more easily digested. Do not cook them in the soak water. For those who have poor digestion or are ill, cook the grain in plenty of fresh water till very soft, almost to gruel consistency. This way you gain most benefit from the grain.

Puffed grains and commercial cereals are highly processed, so limit their use.

Barley

Barley is considered the most acid-forming grain but it has so many good properties that they balance out its use. Whole or sproutable barley contains more fibre, twice the calcium, three times the iron and 25% more protein than pearl barley. Barley is good for the nerves and muscles and it is well worth using whole barley although it does take a little longer to cook. Soaking barley beforehand speeds up cooking time. Cook in the ratio of one cup of barley to four cups of water, for one hour. Soup made with barley and green kale is good for increasing your calcium intake. See the recipe section on page 110.

Bran

Bran is good for red blood cell formation, but can cause constipation if not enough liquid is absorbed during digestion.

Corn

Corn, also called maize, is the most commonly used grain in many countries and fresh corn on the cob has many enzymes and vitamins. It is best not to cook it for more than a few minutes because cooking makes corn a much more starchy vegetable and it is harder to digest. Corn does not contain niacin and should not form the larger part of a diet. It is best in a mixed diet with vegetables.

Millet

Millet is an alkaline-forming grain which cooks quite quickly. Use hulled millet, otherwise you won't be able to cook it soft enough to eat. Millet has a high amino acid and silicon content and can be used frequently by those with celiac problems. Cook one cup of millet to three cups of water for about thirty minutes, after which it can be used in the same way as other grains.

Oats

Oats are rich in silicon and renew bones and connective tissue. They also contain the phosphorous needed by brain and nerve tissues and strengthen cardiac muscles.

Oats are generally thought of in the form of breakfast porridge but they can be used in soups, puddings, breads and savoury loaves. For porridge, cook one cup of rolled oats to five cups of water. Stir occasionally till boiling and simmer for 10—15 minutes, stirring occasionally. The longer they cook the better oats digest and supply nutrients. Refer to the recipe section on page 87.

Rice

Whole brown rice contains a large amount of B vitamins, bran and fibre, as well as the rice germ and its essential oils. It is also very easy to digest if cooked and chewed properly, and can be eaten by those who have allergies to gluten. Made into a gruel, rice is very useful when one is very weak and unable to digest most other foods.

Rice can have almost any other food added to it, savoury or sweet and short grain brown rice is the easiest to use. Rices other than brown rice have been treated and lost much of their nutrient value. Wild rice is not a true rice, it is more in the corn family, but makes a nice change for pilaf and rice salads.

Brown rice can be cooked by several methods. The most common is to add one cup of brown rice to three cups of water, cover and bring to the boil, simmering until the rice is soft, then rinse. According to where the rice was grown (some rice is harder and drier), cook for half to three quarters of an hour, then rinse under running hot or cold water, depending on how the rice is to be used.

Spelt

Spelt is a relative of wheat and has not been used very much until recently. It has mostly been fed to race horses and cattle as a replacement for oats but has now been rediscovered as a beneficial food for humans.

Although coming from the wheat family, spelt can be tolerated by those allergic to wheat, even those with celiac disease and it has a hearty flavour that is lacking in some other grains. Spelt is higher in protein and fat than wheat and its fibre content is water soluble, allowing for better nutrient assimilation by the body.

Spelt is a good grain for those with digestive problems. It comes in the form of whole grain, pastas, flours, cereal and breads. As the grain has a very thick husk, spelt is not usually treated with pesticides or other chemicals.

Wheat

Wheat, eaten in small quantities, is one of the most useful grains as it absorbs a wider range of minerals from the soil than other grains. Unfortunately, most wheat is over-refined and has been genetically altered to resist diseases, which partly explains why some people are allergic to it.

We are constantly exposed to rancid and over-refined wheat products in the production of foods. When grains are milled their oil is exposed to the air and considered rancid.

Pastas

There is a large variety of pastas on the market, made from almost every grain. Those made from wheat are the most acid forming so try using the other grain pastas as wheat is included in many other foods.

Care needs to be taken with the cooking of rice and buckwheat pastas as it is easy to overcook them. A good rule of thumb for most pastas is to cook them *al dente* in plenty of boiling water. Drain and rinse under cold running water and plunge back into a pot of fresh boiling water for 30 seconds just before serving. Pastas are a carbohydrate food and if the body is required to cope with more than it needs, the excess will be stored as fat. Pasta once a week is enough.

Seaweeds

The powers of sea vegetables have been known for centuries. Sea plants contain ten to twenty times the minerals of land plants, and an abundance of vitamins and other properties essential to man. Certain sea vegetables actually remove radioactive and toxic metal wastes from our bodies. They can remove phlegm and clean the lymphatic system. They alkalize the blood, lower cholesterol and fat in the blood, and are beneficial to the thyroid gland. They are excellent sources of calcium, amino acids and iron, varying from ten times to three thousand times, depending on the type of sea vegetable. Until recently, seaweeds were classed as pollution-free because they were generally harvested from pollution-free deep water and they also had the ability to reject toxins, which is part of their incredible usefulness. Nowadays, because of all the toxins dumped into sea water, the pollution-free claim needs to be thoroughly re-examined.

Agar Agar or Kanten

A vegetable gelatin, agar agar does not need refrigeration to set to a firm jelly. It promotes digestion and contains no calories, but has most of the properties of other seaweeds although not quite as much. To use agar agar, add one dessertspoon to a cup of hot liquid, stir and simmer till dissolved. Add to juice to make a jelly or to cooked vegetables to make a terrine or aspic-based mould.

Hijiki or Arame

Hijiki or arame are thread-like lengths of seaweed containing vitamin B2 and niacin. As with other nutrients, they support hormone function. Soak for thirty minutes in warm water and chop. There is no need to cook them. Add to any grain, soup, bread, salad, tofu or vegetable dish.

Kombu and Kelp

Kombu and kelp greatly increase the nutritional value of any food prepared with them as they are considered the most completely mineralised food. Kelp is available in powder or tablet form. It can be used in a salt shaker on the table and, because of its salty flavour, can replace the need for salt in foods.

Kombu and kelp are excellent added to dried beans during cooking, the minerals helping to balance the protein and oils and increasing the digestibility of beans by breaking down the tough fibres. Break or cut the kombu with scissors and add with other ingredients to soup or bean dishes. If using in salads, cook for one hour first.

Nori

Nori fibres are more tender than most seaweeds. It has the highest protein content and is the most easily digested of the seaweed family. It is rich in vitamin A, B and niacin, as well as containing all the other properties, uses and nutrients of seaweeds (refer to charts). Good for goitre and high blood pressure.

Nori comes in sheets and can be eaten as is. It is best to buy toasted nori because it is more tender. It can be used in sushi, crumbled over any food, served hot or cold or in sandwiches, dressings or spreads. Nori dissolves if cooked in hot liquids and will not look good, so it is better to add to soups etc. just before serving.

LIFE IS AN ADVENTURE

Breads

It is worth making your own bread, as many of the so-called wholesome and healthy whole wheat loaves available in the stores are neither. Often, the flour used is mixed whole wheat and processed white, so much of the fibre is lost. Even the distinctive brown colouring may come from caramel. Many such loaves often have as many additives as white bread and are manufactured in much the same way.

When making bread use small amounts of sea salt; sweeteners and oils are not necessary. Make bread in the morning and bake bread at night. On warm sunny days it rises better. Make bread when you feel vital and happy. Your energy will ensure a better loaf (macrobiotic principle).

Bread making machines are very useful in a good nutritional diet as you can use fresh milled flour which retains all the grain nutrients. There is no need to use chemical additives to keep it fresh and you can avoid bakers yeast and use a sour dough culture.

Flours

- Barley flour makes a sticky bread and can be combined 50:50 with whole wheat flour for lightness.
- Brown rice yields a sweeter and smoother bread. Use 20% in combination with other flours.
- Buckwheat makes a good dark, heavy winter bread. Use in combination with wheat and rice flours.
- Chestnut flour gives a light bread. Good combined with small amounts of other flours.
- Cornmeal flour gives a good light bread. Best combined with small amounts of other flours.
- Garbanzo (chickpea) flour can be used alone or mixed with other flours, especially good in sauces and pancakes.
- Kamut flour is light in texture and can be substituted in equal amount for whole wheat pastry flour in cake, pie and muffin recipes.
- Millet flour: always combine with other flour, especially whole wheat (one third millet/two thirds wholewheat).
- Oat flour is light in texture and can be substituted for pastry flour. It adds moistness to cakes and pastries. Add approximately 20% to corn, whole wheat or rice flours.
- Rye flour makes a sticky bread and can be combined 50:50 with rice or whole wheat flour for a lighter bread. 100% rye bread greatly improves in flavour after several days.
- Soy flour, add small amounts to other flours for a smoother and moister texture.
- Spelt flour can be substituted 100% for wheat in bread recipes. Usually well tolerated by those allergic to wheat.

SEE THE JOY IN EVERY EXPERIENCE

Beverages

Plain Water

Plain water is very necessary to life and the recommended quantity varies. We can make some of it more interesting and therapeutic by adding various herbs. There are a huge number of herb teas on the market , but you should avoid drinking one or two of them exclusively as they can have a therapeutic effect. Make sure the kinds you drink are suitable for you (check with a natural therapist before using a particular one on a regular basis and vary them for the properties they contain). Some herb teas are suitable for children. Check with a qualified person who knows your child.

Animal Milks

Animal milks are a necessary choice in some cases and care should be taken to choose the right one. Pasteurisation (the heating of milk to high temperature and cooling rapidly), plus homogenisation (chemically dispersing fat evenly) both have a denuding effect on milk and the products produced from it. Although the original product may contain calcium, it is seriously depleted when these products are pasteurised ie in milk, cheese, canned foods etc.

Bouillon - one teaspoon of mineral bouillon in a cup of hot water is a tasty hot drink instead of soup.

Buttermilk - is good as a laxative.

Coconut milk - (made from the flesh of the coconut) is quite nutritious but a high-fat food so needs to be used sparingly.

Goat's milk - fresh or in dried whey, supplies potassium, sodium phosphate and calcium.

Grain and nut milk - are very nutritious and suitable to be used in smoothies and desserts.

Nut milk was made and used centuries ago. Europeans made almond and walnut milk, Arabs made almond milk, Indians made coconut milk and the Chinese made a soybean milk. Native Americans made milk from pecan and .

Soy milk

Research shows that although some soy milk is fortified with calcium, the system only absorbs about 75% of that calcium, which is less than the calcium absorbed from cow's milk. Soy milk is still a good source of protein, B vitamins and iron and is free of lactose. Best used when diluted 2:1 with water as soy milk is quite "heavy" and contains fairly high quantities of protein, which can be hard on digestion processes (possibly dehydrating, as protein requires liquid to digest).

GRAIN CONSUMPTION IN MEAT PRODUCTION

Approximately 8 kilograms of grain and soy are needed to produce ½ kilo of edible food from a cow.

Seven people could be fed for a whole year on the grain soy needed to produce the meat and poultry eaten by the average person in one year.

Soy Products

Miso - is a fermented paste made from soy beans, grains and mould (*koji*).
There are three basic types of miso :
• soybean (*hatcho*)
• barley (*mugi*)
• rice (*kome*), as well as many variations.

Miso contains amino acids, protein, traces of vitamin B12 and is a live food containing lactobacillus bacteria. It creates an alkaline condition in the body that promotes resistance to disease.

Most of the nutrients in miso are destroyed by boiling, so add the paste to soups and stews just before serving. A teaspoon of miso dissolved in a cup of hot water has the ability to settle an upset stomach by creating an alkaline environment. It helps too when you have overeaten or are undergoing chemotherapy. Because it adds a hearty flavour, miso is sometimes overused by people when changing to a meatless diet. Be aware that it is stronger than meat because of its ageing and sea salt content. When used in moderation, it provides excellent nutrition. You can add it to stews, soups, gravies, sauces, dressings, stuffings, dips and spread sparingly on toast.

Soy beans - are very alkalizing and can be a valuable food. They help remove toxins from the body and provide phyto-oestrogens and trytophan. But soy beans are the hardest bean to digest, and, unless very well cooked, inhibit digestive enzymes. The fermentation process, such as that used in the making of tempeh, tofu, miso and soy sauce, eliminates the trypsin effect of the soybean. This process also makes them easier to assimilate and so it is better to use these products than to use whole unprocessed soybeans.

Soy milk - there are many soy milks on the market. Choose one that is made from organic whole soy beans and use it in moderation. This will provide protein and calcium and can be used in the same way as cow's milk (except for small children). There is oat milk and rice milk as well. These products are good to use as they do not cause the digestive problems that can arise from using cow's milk.

Soy yoghurt - has many of the same nutritional properties as cow's milk yoghurt, except lacto bacillus, but has the added benefits of the soybean.

Tempeh - originating in Indonesia, this fermented food is made from cooked soybean bound together by a mould. There are many flavours and varieties. Asian tempeh can be a good source of vitamin B12 but, when made in Western countries, the B12 content is not as high because of the clean environment of the manufacturing area, so B12 is often injected into the finished product. Tempeh must be cooked either by baking, steaming or boiling, and is improved by marinating, as is tofu.

Tofu - is a processed soybean curd that originated in China thousands of years ago, and developed to improve the digestibility of the valued soybean. Tofu contains protein, B vitamins and minerals, and a calcium content equal to that of cow's milk. We do not need a lot of tofu but it is a versatile product which can be baked, steamed, boiled, sautéed and even eaten raw (because of its blandness it soaks up whatever flavouring it is put with). To store, cover with water, keep in an airtight container/jar in a cool place and change the water daily.

Oils and Fats

There are three types of oil or fat:

Saturated
Solid at room temperature and primarily from animal sources, but including coconut, peanut, palm and cottonseed.

Mono-unsaturated
Olive and sesame, canola and avocado. Liquid at room temperature, solid when cold.

Polyunsaturated
Flax, soy and walnut must not be heated. Liquid at room temperature and also when cold; comes from the vegetable kingdom.

Some fat or oil is essential to the digestion of our food and it provides a satisfying effect when we eat. For most people the savoury taste of fried food is very pleasant.

Our earliest ancestors ate the meat and the fat that was naturally in that meat when it was cooked. It was a natural accompaniment. The amount of fat was in balance with the meat, as the animal grew that way. The difference with today's meat is that it is not grown naturally. Cattle can be fed a combination of chemicals and what is not excreted is stored in the fat of the animal in very concentrated amounts. Added to all the other allowed chemicals in our food, it is no wonder people are getting sicker at a younger age. If you can manage, it is good to have high quality, low fat meat only once or twice a week — just a smallish portion to satisfy your needs. Meat has some nutrients that are not easy to obtain from other sources, B12 and iron are just two and animal phosphorus is needed in very small quantities for good brain function.

Protein is in good supply from other foods. The needed fat is better taken from a vegetable source, like flax or olives.

Flax and olive oil can be obtained cold-pressed, meaning the oil has not been extracted with heat and/or chemicals. When the oils are cold-pressed they retain all their nutrients, especially omega 3, which is essential for us. We need only a very small amount of Omega 6 and 9.

If possible, buy unrefined oils in dark glass containers or light-free cans, as light causes the oil to lose most of its nutritional properties. Oils labeled cold-extracted and unrefined only retain their nutritional properties if they are used cold.

Most other oils are extracted by high heat and, as such, are useless nutrient-wise and, in some cases, quite harmfully out of balance. Flax oil should never be heated as it loses its beneficial properties (and tastes unpleasant). You can add flax oil to dressings cold, or take from a spoon, in a juice, or poured over food just before eating. If you need to cook with oil use olive oil at a ratio of 50:50 with water to saute vegetables or pan fry foods, as the water stops the oil heating to the carcinogenic point.

Use unsalted butter to grease a cooking pan as oil sprays are loaded with chemicals. Also use unsalted butter in cakes or desserts instead of oils as heated oil is worse for us than butter. If you need to deep-fry food use the oil only once and drain the food well on absorbent paper. Cakes and desserts can be made without fat of any kind, they are just a little dryer in texture and don't keep in an edible state for very long.

The right types of fat, or fatty acids more correctly, are necessary in our diet and are needed for the normal growth of children. We need a small amount of mono-unsaturated and a slightly larger amount of polyunsaturated fat. Once converted into fatty acid these fats and oils are used in cellular function, are involved in metabolic processes, are needed by hormones to regulate body processes, and are burned for energy.

We can function very well without saturated fats, which are the cheapest to manufacture and are used for most deep-fried food, in bakery goods, and in many prepared foods.

Mono-unsaturated and polyunsaturated fats are both useful in the system and are derived from plants. The chemical action with regard to nutrition is quite difficult to understand but there are properties in both that we need in balance. Mono-unsaturated oils contain a predominance of omega 6, 9 and some 3. The most common of these are safflower, sunflower, canola and olive oil. When heated and used for cooking they should be used only once and discarded.

Seasonings

Liquid bouillons and dried organic vegetable powders can provide added flavour in your soups, sauces and casseroles. Miso, tamari and soy are useful, as are fresh herbs and spices. Natural yeast powders can also help with flavour while adding extra nutrients. These seasonings are a better choice to use in your food as most of the generally used ones are chemically formulated.

Tamari
A naturally made and aged soy sauce, twice as strong as commercially made soy sauce - nutritious as it is made from soy beans.

Herbamare
Powdered organic vegetables and herbs - can be sprinkled on food and used in cooking.

Sea Salt
Natural organic sea salt contains many essential minerals - use sparingly in cooking.

Braggs Bouillon
A brown, strong, mineral liquid especially suited to flavouring soups, sauces and casseroles. Nutritious and pleasant tasting as a hot drink.

WE ARE WHAT WE ARE BECAUSE OF OUR THINKING

EVERYONE AND EVERYTHING AROUND YOU IS YOUR TEACHER

Ken Keyes Jnr.

Vegetables

Vegetables cleanse the body and purify the blood. Lightly cooked vegetables retain most of their vitamins and minerals, while long, slow cooking is necessary for some of the root vegetables and are better digested by those with compromised digestive systems.

Asparagus
- supplies iodine, chlorine, sulphur, vitamin E, potassium and phosphorous
- a good tonic for the kidneys
- break off and discard the tough stem and boil or steam the rest for 7-8 minutes to remove a slightly toxic chemical

Beetroot
- supplies magnesium, potassium, manganese and sodium
- good for liver ailments, improves circulation and purifies the blood
- beetroot is an 'eliminating' food
- organic tastes better
- boil whole and serve hot or cold or, to serve raw, scrub and grate, adding a little dressing

Broccoli
- supplies calcium, phosphorous, magnesium, iron, sulphur, vitamins A and B5, and more vitamin C than citrus
- if cooked lightly will retain all its chlorophyll content which reduces its gas-forming properties

Brussel Sprouts
- supply sulphur, potassium, phosphorous and many vitamins and minerals
- high fibre content, helps the bowels to work well
- contains sulforaphane, which helps the body to fight carcinogens
- although they look and taste like little cabbages they are far more valuable

Cabbage
- supplies chlorine, sulphur, chlorophyll, iodine, calcium, vitamin E and more vitamin C than citrus
- benefits all stomach problems
- 40% more calcium in green cabbage than white cabbage
- purifies the blood and deters constipation

Capsicum
- supplies iodine, bioflavonoids and vitamin C

Carrots
- supply calcium, phosphorous, magnesium, chlorine and vitamin A
- alkaline forming, which helps to clear acidic blood conditions
- one of the richest sources of vitamin A, an anti-oxidant that protects against cancer
- stimulates the release of wastes and clears intestinal tract
- dissolves tumours and growths

Cauliflower

- supplies potassium, biotin, iron, and vitamin C.
- contains large quantities of sulforaphane.
- high fibre content.
- helps keep the body fluids balanced.
- helps the heart function and blood pressure.

Celery

- supplies chlorine, insulin, chlorophyll and magnesium.
- reduces acids and adds essential sodium (as distinct from salt)
- improves digestion and liver function
- high in silicon (helps to renew bones, arteries and all connective tissue)
- a few stalks eaten raw will satisfy salt cravings
- helps to reduce high blood pressure

Corn

- supplies chlorine, calcium, phosphorous, manganese and folic acid
- starch in yellow sweet corn is very easy to digest
- has one of the best fibres for our bowel
- a great bone and muscle builder
- soup made from barley and corn is very high in magnesium and is excellent for the nervous system and brain

Cucumber

- supplies sodium, silica, chlorine and bromine
- counteracts toxins and cleanses the blood
- reduces acids and adds sodium
- acts as a digestive aid and cools the system in summer
- juice is good for kidney and bladder problems
- contains an enzyme – erepsis – that breaks down protein and cleanses the intestines
- can be used raw or cooked

Eggplant

- one cup of steamed eggplant supplies 31 mg of iron, equal to 1 kg of beef or 10 hamburgers
- is full of vitamins and minerals

Edible Flowers

- apple or any fruit flower, borage, clover, lavender, marigold, rose, rosemary, violet, zucchini and hibiscus

Garlic

- supplies sulphur.
- very useful for promoting circulation
- eliminates unfavourable bacteria in yeasts
- improves healthy bacteria in the intestines and eliminates many toxins from the body.
- eats cholesterol on artery walls (see also onions)

Green String Beans
- supply phosphorous, manganese and nitrogen
- good nerve and body builder
- helps with diabetes

Lettuce
- supplies silicon, iron, copper, chlorophyll, biotin, potassium and chlorine
- green leafy lettuce is much richer in nutrients than head lettuce
- contains chlorophyll (plus iron, vitamins A and C) in the outer green leaves
- try not to use hydroponically grown lettuce (or other produce grown this way) as the chemicals used to grow them are concentrated in the recycled water.
  Even if it is a natural fertilizer it can become too concentrated.

Mushrooms
- supply selenium, bromine and silica
- contains antibiotic properties
- increases immunity against disease
- increases the appetite while decreasing fat levels in the blood
- reduces mucus in the respiratory tract

Olives
- supply sodium, calcium and phosphorous
- black olives supply the highest source of potassium (rinse off brine)
- good brain and nerve food

Onions
- supply potassium, phosphorous, iodine and silicon
- rich in sulphur, which purifies the body and cleans the arteries
- helps remove heavy metals from the body
- helps to keep the blood at a viscous level – avoids clotting (see also garlic)

Parsnip
- supplies potassium, phosphorous, choline and sulphur
- good for spleen and pancreas
- helps avoid blood clotting
- benefits the stomach, liver and gall bladder
- best used cooked in soups and stews or dry baked in the oven

Parsley
- supplies vitamin A and C, calcium, potassium, iron, chlorophyll, sodium and magnesium
- improves digestion
- useful in treatment of ear infection
- strengthens adrenals
- good for brain and optic nerve
- effective in treatment of kidney and urinary difficulties
  Note : not to be used by nursing mothers as it can dry up milk.

Peas

- supply phosphorous, potassium, iron and manganese
- good source of vitamin E (not frozen peas)
- good for bone formation and healthy nerves
- help kidney function

Potatoes

- supply potassium, magnesium, sulphur, iodine, chlorine
- cook with skin on to retain their essential nutrients

Pumpkin

- supplies silicon, potassium and iron
- helps regulate blood sugar levels
- can help bronchial problems
- use cooked: boil, bake, steam, mash or use in casseroles and stews

Radishes

- supply potassium and choline
- good for detoxifying the body
- reduce mucus and help reduce viral infection

Spinach/Silverbeet

- supplies iron and chlorophyll
- useful source of vitamin A
- wash carefully and steam or boil
- very small amounts can be eaten raw as they contain oxalic acid

Sweet Potato/Yams

- supply vitamin A
- remove toxins from the body
- good mixed with pumpkin in a soup or sliced and baked in the oven

Tomato

- supplies chlorine, sulphur, potassium, sodium and lycopene
- fresh tomato can help to cleanse the body
- stimulates production of gastric juices for protein digestion.

*Much study has been done regarding the difference in the food value
of vegetables, comparing fresh with frozen.*

*One of the advantages of crisp fresh vegetables is the ingestion of
the life force or energy of that vegetable.
This life force is missing when vegetables are frozen.
On the other hand, however, it is better to have snap-frozen vegetables than
a limp dead vegetable that has been on the shelf for a long time.
Organic vegetables provide the advantage of your body not having to deal
with pesticides or chemical sprays.*

Fruit

We are conditioned from an early age to eat lots of fruit. Much of the fruit that we eat is picked before it is properly ripe and it does not develop the expected nutrients until the sun actually ripens it. When ripening or getting soft unnaturally it contains a lot of sugar which is destructive to the immune system and as such the fruit is not as nutritious as it should be. Buy organic fruit for the best nutritional value.

Drinking a lot of sweet fruit juice can be very weakening and may promote the growth of yeasts in the body. Fruit is generally considered not to mix well with other food during digestion as fruit digests faster and starts to ferment in the stomach while waiting for the rest of the food to be processed.

It is better to have a fruit meal on an empty stomach, ie. breakfast or mid-afternoon. Eat whole fruits rather than juices. Fruit juices should not be drunk with a meal.

Apples
- supply vitamins A, C and E, biotin and folic acid
- one of the most useful fruits, apples contain pectin and help to clear cholesterol
- the malic acid clears harmful bacteria in the digestive tract
- the fruit and juice are beneficial for the liver and gall bladder

Apricots
- supply vitamins A, phosphorous, iron and manganese
- useful for those with anemia
- helps with lung problems such as asthma
- high in cobalt and copper
- limit apricots if you tend to have trouble with diarrhoea

Avocado
- supply biotin, folic acid, calcium, potassium, sodium and magnesium
- natural source of lecithin and monosaturated fats/oils
- a good protein
- rich in copper, which helps build red blood cells

Bananas
- supply manganese, potassium, iron, copper, biotin and magnesium
- good for reducing blood pressure because of high potassium content
- treats hypertension
- steamed bananas are good for reducing diarrhoea, colitis and haemorrhoids
- calms the body system for cellular electrolyte balance
- very sweet, making a great sugar substitute when used as a puree

Cherries

- supply copper and manganese
- high in easily assimilated iron
- good for gout and arthritis as they help eliminate excess body acid
- try to obtain organic cherries as most commercially grown ones are very heavily sprayed

Figs

- supply iron, calcium and potassium
- a very alkalizing fruit, can help balance acid conditions resulting from a diet high in meat and refined foods
- good for cleansing the bowel (constipation)

Grapefruit

- supplies biotin, phosphorous, potassium and magnesium
- similar properties to lemons but not as useful

Grapes

- supply manganese, silicon and folic acid
- red grapes in particular, are good blood builders
- improve the cleansing function of our glands
- help with liver problems such as hepatitis and jaundice
- the juice improves kidney function

Lemons

- supply phosphorous, sodium and calcium
- all citrus fruits have a small amount of vitamin C
- help with digestion and are particularly cleansing
- clean the blood and help circulation
- benefit liver and absorption of minerals
- reduce flatulence
- calm the nerves
- a little juice in water first thing in the morning helps to destroy bad bacteria in the mouth and intestines and encourages the production of bile by improving liver function

Oranges

- supply calcium, phosphorous and magnesium
- best eaten as a whole fruit and not as a juice
- usually sprayed very heavily and picked while still green
- can be quite acidic due to growing and picking procedures

Pawpaw

- supplies calcium, potassium, iron and magnesium
- particularly good for treating indigestion or if you have eaten too much protein

Pears

- supply folic acid, silicon, potassium and iron
- beneficial for constipation problems
- help cleanse the lungs of mucus
- eat whole or have the juice first thing in the morning

Pineapple

- supplies manganese
- contains the enzyme bromelin, which can help to increase digestive ability

Prunes

- supply iron, sodium and magnesium
- have the highest content of nerve salts (tissue salts that strengthen the nerves)
- full of minerals and help regulate acid/alkaline balance

Raspberries

- supply iron and silicon
- thought to be beneficial in the treatment of some types of cancer

Strawberries

- supply choline and sulphur
- rich in silicon
- good for spleen and pancreas
- eat before a meal as they can stimulate the appetite
- a good spring cleanser (helps clear the system of any accumulations of the heavier winter foods)
- organic, if possible, because they are one of the most highly sprayed fruits

Almonds

- are a protein food
- contain a good quantity of calcium
- supply monounsaturated fatty acid (to keep cholesterol in check)
- more benefit is obtained from almonds if they are soaked in cold water for about 12 hours

Peanuts

- are actually a bean, not a nut – some children are allergic to peanuts, they contain aflotoxins, a mild poison

Most other nuts have a high fat content and are best eaten straight after shelling, as the oil/fat starts to oxidize (go rancid) as soon as the air comes in contact with the unprotected oil. Nuts can also be very difficult for children to digest. While they are usually good nutrition they should be freshly ground and added to a child's food.

Nutrient Content Charts (except where noted *- 100 gram portions)

FOOD	Protein gr.	Carbohydrates mg	Calcium mg	Iron mg	Saturated Fat gr	Digestion Times hrs	Acid/Alkaline	Vitamins
Agar Agar*50 grm	2.5	75	200	2.5	-	1.5	Alk	E
Almonds	20	20	200	4.5	-	2.25	Alk	AB
Apple *1	.5	24	12	.5	-	2.75	Alk	ABC
Apricot *3	1	13	18	5	-	2.75	Alk	BC
Asparagus	1	1.5	21	6	-	2.25	Alk	ABC
Alfalfa	5.5	-	28	2.5	-	2	Alk	AB
Avocado	2	6.5	10	5	-	1.75	Alk	ABC
Banana *1	1	20	12	1	-	3	Alk	ABC
Barley	8	80	26	2	-	4	Acid	B

Bread: *1 slice
  Wholewheat
  White-enriched
	
	2.5
	2
		
		11
		11
			
			23
			24
				
				5
				6
					
					.11
					18
						
						3
						4
							
							Acid
							Acid
								
								ABmin
								B's

Broccoli	2.5	3.5	70	1	-	3	Alk	ABC
Butter	75	.2	23	-	50	3.25	Acid	ADE
Beef	18	-	10	3	4	3.5	Acid	E
Brussel Sprouts	1	5	14	.5	-	4	Alk	ABC
Cabbage	1.5	7	16	.5	-	3	Alk	ABE
Carob Powder	4	60	200	3	-	3	Alk	-
Carrot	1	10	37	.75	-	2.25	Alk	ABCD
Capsicum	1.5	7	16	.5	-	3	Alk	ABC
Cauliflower	3	5	26	1	-	2.25	Alk	ABC

Nutrient Content Charts (except where noted *- 100 gram portions)

FOOD	Protein gr.	Carbohydrates mg.	Calcium mg	Iron mg.	Saturated Fat gr.	Digestion Times hrs.	Acid/Alkaline	Vitamins
Celery	1	4.5	47	.5	-	3.25	Alk	ABC
Chickpeas	21	62	300	11	.5	3	Acid	BE
Corn	3	25	2.5	.5	-	3	Alk	ABC
Coconut	.5	33	9	1	20	3.25	Acid	ABC
Cucumber	1	3.5	26	1	-	3.25	Alk	ABC
Chicken	12	-	8	1	2	3.25	Acid	E
Cheese:								
Parmesan	9	80	320	20	3	3	Acid	AB
Cottage	13	3	62	14	3	3	Acid	ABCD
Hard	21	210	560	100	18	3	Acid	AB
Dates	2	72	60	3	-	2.5	Alk	ABC
Eggs *1	5.5	.4	24	1	1.5	2.25	Acid	ABE
Fish:								
White/Deep-sea	22	-	10	.5	.25	3	Acid	ABE
Flour:								
Rice	7.5	107	11	6.5	-	3	Acid	ABE
Rye	8	70	20	10	-	3.25	Acid	AB
Soy	43	36	260	9	18	3	Acid	AB
Wholewheat	11.8	9.7	18	.9	-	3	Acid	BDE
Garlic *1 clove	-	.5	-	.5	-	2	Alk	ABC
Grapes	1.5	18	20	.5	-	1.5	Alk	ABC
Green Bean	1	6.5	30	2	-	3.25	Alk	ABC

Nutrient Content Charts (except where noted *- 100 gram portions)

FOOD	Protein gr.	Carbohydrates mg.	Calcium mg	Iron mg.	Saturated Fat gr.	Digestion Times hrs.	Acid/Alkaline	Vitamins
Seaweed:								
Nori *2 sheets	2.2	2	13	.5	-	1.5	Alk	ABC
Hijiki *50 grm	5.5	42	6	2.7	-	1.25	Alk	ABCE
Kombu *50grm	7.5	54	400	5	-	1.5	Alk	ABCE
Kelp *1 tbs	1.5	5.5	156	.5	-	1.25	Alk	ABCE
Lamb	12	-	7	.5	7-10	2	Acid	AB
Leek	2	11	52	1	-	2.5	Alk	ABCE
Lemon *1 tbs	-	1.2	-	1	-	2	Alk	BC
Lentil	19	18	27	3	-	3	Acid	AB
Lettuce	1	3	74	1.5	-	2.25	Alk	ABCE
Lima Bean	8	25	24	4	-	2.25	Alk	BE
Melon (water)	.5	6	7	.5	-	2	Alk	ABC
Milk:								
Cow	3.75	5	130	5.5	2.5	2	Alk	ABCE
Goat	4	5	160	6	3.5	2	Alk	ABCE
Soy	7.7	5	47	1.5	-	2.5	Alk	BC
Whey 10 grm	120	6	60	.075	.075	2	Alk	ABC
Miso *50 grm	48	107	128	1	-	2	Alk	AB
Millet	11	80	20	7	-	3	Alk	A
Mung Bean Sprouts 1 cup	3	6	14	.9				
Mushroom	2	3	18	3	-	2.5	Alk	AB
Shiitake 100 grm	0.5	0.5			1			
Oats	2	10	11	.5	-	2.5	Alk	ABE
Olives (black)	1	30	100	1.5	-	1.75	Alk	AE

38

Nutrient Content Charts (except where noted *- 100 gram portions)

FOOD	Protein gr.	Carbohydrates mg.	Calcium mg	Iron mg.	Saturated Fat gr.	Digestion Times hrs.	Acid/Alkaline	Vitamins
Onion	1	7	85	1.5	-	3.25	Alk	AE
Orange	1	16	-	-	-	2	Alk	ABCDE
Olive Oil *1 tbs	.5	.5	-	-	1.5	3.25	Alk	ADE
Parsley	4	10	275	7	-	1.5	Alk	B
Parsnip	2	18	50	.5	-	3	Alk	AB
Pasta (wholewheat)	4	32	8	1	-	3	Acid	BE
Pecans	4.5	7	40	1	4	3	Acid	AB
Peas	6	16	18	1.5	-	3.5	Alk	ABC
Peach	.5	10	9	.5	-	2.25	Acid	ABC
Pear	.75	15	8	.2	-	2.25	Acid	B
Potato	2	16	7	.5	-	2	Alk	ABC
Prune	1.5	50	42	3.5	-	3	Acid	AB
Pumpkin	1	10	26	.5	-	3.25	Alk	ABC
Pineapple	.5	21	-	-	-	2	Alk	ABC
Radish	1	3	28	.5	-	3.25	Alk	BC
Rice	2	20	10	.5	-	2	Acid	ABE
Rice - (wild)	3.2		2.5	0.5				
Salmon	22	-	260	1.5	1	3.75	Acid	ABC
Sardine	24	-	50	.5	1	3	Acid	AB
Silver beet	2	4	90	2	-	3	Alk	ABCD

Nutrient Content Charts (except where noted *- 100 gram portions)

FOOD	Protein gr.	Carbohydrates mg.	Calcium mg	Iron mg.	Saturated Fat gr.	Digestion Times hrs.	Acid/Alkaline	Vitamins
Soy Beans	28.6	17	175	8.8	2.2		Alk	
Spinach	2.5	3	80	2	-	2	Alk	ABCD
Spring Onion	0.3	2	4	0.1				
Sweet Potato	1	18	23	.5	-	3.25	Alk	ABC
Sugar	-	1(simple)	-	-	-	1.5	Acid	B
Tofu	8	3	250	4	-	3	Alk	B
Tomato	1	7	20	.5	-	2	Acid(raw) Alk(cooked)	ABC
Tomato Paste- sundried	5	25	46	3.9	.2			
Tuna	28	-	16	1.5	-	3	Acid	AB
Yoghurt	4	5.5	135	.5	2.5	2	Alk	AB
Walnut	7	7	45	1.5	2.5	3	Acid	B
Zucchini	.75	2.5	-	.5	-	2.75	Alk	A

Miscellaneous Flavourings

FOOD	Protein gr.	Carbohydrates mg.	Calcium mg	Iron mg.	Saturated Fat gr.	Digestion Times hrs.	Acid/Alkaline	Vitamins
Honey 1 tsp	0.1		1	0.1			Acid	
Soy Mayonnaise 2 tbs	.07	.3			1.7			
Cream Dairy ½ cup		2.5		75	0.35			Acid
Torula (yeast) 100 grm	38.6		424	19.3				
Braggs Bouillon	9.5				.07			

Nutrient Content Charts (except where noted *- 100 gram portions)

FOOD	Protein gr.	Carbohydrates mg.	Calcium mg	Iron mg.	Saturated Fat gr.	Digestion Times hrs.	Acid/Alkaline	Vitamins
Tamari 1 tbs	1.2		2.4	0.3	1.0			
Ginger fresh 1tsp	0.1		0.1					
Tahini 1tsp	2.6		64	1.3				
Basil dried 1 tsp	0.2		30	0.6				
Coriander dried 1tsp	0.2		13	0.3				
Oregano dried 1 tsp	0.2		24	.7				
Rosemary dried 1tsp	0.1		15	0.4				
Curry Powder	0.3		10	0.6				
Parsley	0.1		4	0.3				

Note: ¼ tsp dried herbs = 1 tsp fresh herbs
         2 tsp dried yeast = 1 oz compressed fresh yeast

No reliable reference is available where no figure appears in this chart.
These tables were cross-referenced from -   • Nutritional Almanac, USA
                                            • Laugh with Health, Aust
                                            • Bernard Jensen, Healing Foods, USA
as they all differed in the nutrient content of each food.

Foods and Tips to Boost the Immune System

All grains in their natural form – not processed
The nutrients needed are contained in the outer husk or shell. Barley, rice, millet, spelt and oats.

Green leafy vegetables
The usefulness of these is the chlorophyll in the green part. It cleans and rebuilds blood and cells.

Sea vegetables
Sea vegetables have lots of protein, calcium, minerals and chlorophyll. Nori, kombu and arame are some. Sushi is a good way to eat this.

Carrots
Carrots have a nutrient called beta-carotene, or vitamin A, which blocks the production of malignant cells. Carrot juice gives a big boost to immunity.

All fresh vegetable juices are useful.

Sprouts
Alfalfa, in particular, is extra helpful to the immune system, providing many vitamins, minerals, enzymes and protein.

Broccoli, cabbage and brussel sprouts help.

Nuts and seeds – not peanuts
As fresh as possible, not roasted are best. Can use nut spreads instead of butter. Definitely don't use margarine as it contains oils that are damaging to the immune system.

Add omega 3 oil to the diet
Fish is a good way to get this but there are tablets and capsules available that come from flax seed.

Shiitake mushrooms
Dried or fresh, shiitake mushrooms contain a chemical compound called lentinen that has been proven to boost the activity of the immune system immensely.

Organic produce
Where possible buy organic foods, particularly vegetables and fruit, so that the immune system doesn't have to deal with the possibly harmful sprays used commercially to grow vegetables.

Limit your sugar intake as sugar in all forms, even fruit, lowers the immune system. Even fruit juices are very high in sugar.

Fried foods put a heavy fat load into your system that makes it very hard for your cells to absorb oxygen and to rebuild effectively.

Eat simple meals and get some exercise – walking is one of the best.

As there are very few nutrients in processed foods, they are best avoided or at least severely limited.

Additives to Avoid

The following list includes those additives in food products that are known to have links with intolerant reactions. While it is vital to avoid these ingredients if your child appears hyperactive, has problems with asthma or eczema, or is sensitive to aspirin, I feel that they should if possible be excluded from the diet of all babies and children.

ARTIFICIAL COLOURS

E102	Tartrazine
E104	Quinoline Yellow
E107	Yellow 2G
E110	Sunset Yellow
E120	Cochineal
E122	Carnosine
E123	Amaranth
E124	Ponceau 4R
E127	Erythrosine
E128	Red 2G
E132	Indigo Carmine
E133	Brilliant Blue
E150	Caramel
E151	Black PN
E154	Brown FK
E155	Chocolate Brown HT

NATURAL COLOUR

E160b   Annatto

ANTI-OXIDANTS
- used to extend the life of some processed packaged foods.

E211	Sodium Benzoate
E310	Propyl gallate
E311	Octyl gallate
E312	Dodecyl gallate
E320	Butylated hydroxyanisole
E321	Butylated hydroxytoluene

FLAVOUR ENHANCERS

621	Sodium hydrogen L-glutamate (Monosodium glutamate; MSG)
622	Potassium hydrogen L-glutamate
623	Calcium dihydrogen di-L-glutamte
627	Guanosine 5''-(disodium phosphate)
631	Ompsome 5''-(disodium phosphate)
635	Sodium 5''-ribonucleotide

SWEETENER

951   Aspartane - generally used to sweeten products labelled 'sugar-free'
- can have potentially damaging side-effects

PRESERVATIVE

220	Sulphur Dioxide
282	Calcium Propionate

SOURCES

Maurice Hansen, *E for Additives* (1984, Guilford and Kings Lynn, Thorsons) pp 12-13.

The London Food Commission, *Food Adulteration and How to Beat It* (1998, London, Unwin Paperbacks).

43

Recommended Daily Intake of Nutrients
(National Academy of Science and Nutrition USA)

Child Age	Protein (Gram)	Calcium (Milligram)	Iron (Milligram)	Fats (Gram)
6 months -1 year: Kg X	2	425	10	-
1-3 years	23	800	15	38
4-6 years	30	800	10	58
7-10 years	34	800	10	80

Protein	= 4 Calories per gram
Carbohydrates	= 4 Calories per gram
Fat	= 9 Calories per gram

The 12 Body Systems

- *Respiratory*
- *Digestive*
- *Circulatory*
- *Nervous*
- *Skeletal*
- *Muscular*
- *Immune*
- *Endocrine*
- *Integument*
- *Urinary*
- *Excretory*
- *Reproductive*

Respiratory System

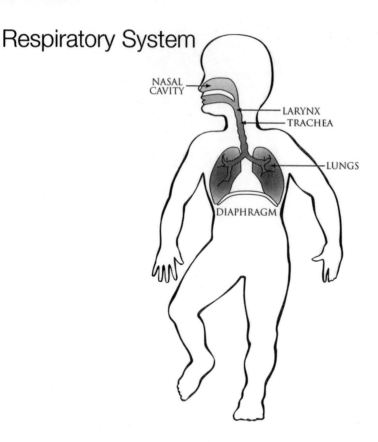

NASAL CAVITY

LARYNX
TRACHEA

LUNGS

DIAPHRAGM

The complete set of structures that are **the respiratory system** are the nose, mouth, oesophagus (throat), trachea (windpipe) bronchial tubes and the lungs.

Every organ in the body needs oxygen to stay alive. We breathe in air through the mouth and nose and it passes down the throat and along the bronchi to the lungs where it is captured in air sacs. Air goes through the walls of the sacs and capillaries into the blood tissue, where some of it is used for energy production and then carbon-dioxide is produced.

The blood stream carries this carbon-dioxide back to the lungs to be breathed out.

Specific nutrients needed to nourish this system:
• Vitamins: A, all Bs, C, D, E, inositol, niacin, folic acid, pantothenic acid and bioflavanoids
• Minerals: calcium, iron, silicon, potassium, magnesium and copper
• Foods: onion family, garlic, green leafy vegetables, grapes, pears and pineapple
Juices to help: • Celery • Watercress • Apple • Carrot

Digestive System

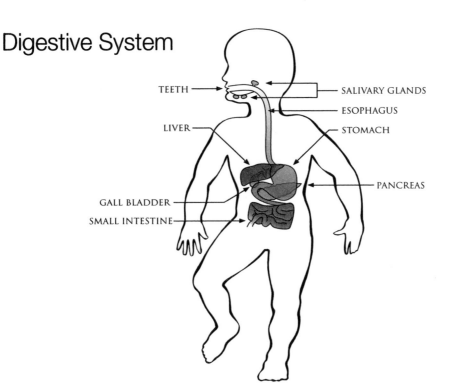

TEETH
SALIVARY GLANDS
ESOPHAGUS
LIVER
STOMACH
PANCREAS
GALL BLADDER
SMALL INTESTINE

The digestive system consists of the mouth, throat (oesophagus), stomach, duodenum and small intestine. The function of the digestive system is to make use of our food and it is essentially a complicated length of tubing. Digestion also involves the liver, gall bladder and pancreas. We are consciously only in control of putting food in our mouth, chewing and swallowing it; the process after that is automatic until the body is ready to get rid of the food we don't need.

Before food can be used by the body it needs to be broken down into a simple chemical form. We put food in our mouth and chew it, and it then passes down the oesophagus as a chyme to the stomach where it stays for several hours. The action of the stomach acids and enzymes starts the breakdown of proteins and carbohydrates. The chyme is then forced into the duodenum where fats are acted upon by bile, which is sent to the duodenum from the liver, gall bladder and pancreas. The food then passes into another section of the small intestine where the digestive process is finished. The nutrients from our food are absorbed into the blood through the velli in this part of the small intestine and the balance of the food not needed goes to the large intestine (or bowel).

Although the digestive system is a marvellous process, we need to be aware of the types of food we eat in order to obtain the best possible nutrition. Continually eating a limited variety of vegetables, grains and fruit is not giving our bodies the best chance of remaining healthy.

Our emotions also play a large part in the digestion of food. Being happy, calm and enjoying the look of what we are about to eat helps us gain more from our meal. Foods are acid or alkaline in our body. We need 75% alkaline foods and 25% acid. When our food is too acid we are allowing disease to enter.

Specific nutrients needed to nourish this system
• Vitamins: A, all Bs, C, D, E, F, folic acid, inositol, niacin and pantothenic acid
• Minerals: magnesium, potassium, iron, sulphur, copper and zinc
• Foods: Lots of green leafy vegetables, watercress, beetroot and some soured milk products eg. yoghurt

Juices to help: • Papaya • Carrot • Whey
• Chlorophyll

Circulatory System

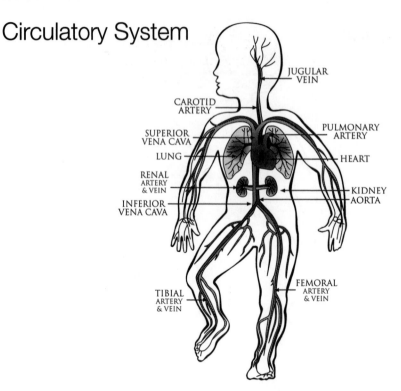

JUGULAR VEIN

CAROTID ARTERY

SUPERIOR VENA CAVA

LUNG

RENAL ARTERY & VEIN

INFERIOR VENA CAVA

PULMONARY ARTERY

HEART

KIDNEY
AORTA

TIBIAL ARTERY & VEIN

FEMORAL ARTERY & VEIN

The circulatory system comprises the heart, blood vessels and the blood. Blood is pumped through the circulatory system by the action of the heart. The supply of blood is necessary for every organ and tissue to remain alive. This supply occurs with the blood's continuous circulation through arteries, capillaries and veins. The artery walls are thickest because they have to withstand the fairly high pressure of the blood being pumped from the heart. Millions of red cells are made every second in the bone marrow, penetrating the bones' capillary walls, to be sent via the blood around the body. Exchange of gases, food and waste take place through capillaries, while the kidneys are the filter organ of the body, helping to keep the blood clean by transporting waste matter from the body. A decision has never been made as to where circulation begins, so to follow its route we will start with the right ventricle, from which blood is forced to the lungs after travelling through the whole circulatory system and depositing oxygen in all tissues as it goes.

When it arrives in the lungs, the blood is now ready to take up more oxygen while releasing carbon dioxide, which we breathe out.

After picking up oxygen from the lungs, the blood travels back into the left side of the heart, the left ventricle, where at the next beat of the heart it is pumped into the aorta and all its bronchi and back around the body. Our red blood cells and some of our white cells and blood platelets are made in our bone marrow. Nearly all bones are involved in making blood cells. Other white cells are made in the lymphatic system and in the spleen. The white cells are concerned with immunity. In a young child nearly all the blood cells are made in bone marrow, but in an adult there are generally only a few bones involved: the spine, ribs, breastbone, pelvis and upper parts of the arm and leg bones.

Specific nutrients needed to nourish this system :
• Vitamins: all Bs, E, folic acid and bioflavonoid
• Minerals: calcium, iron, silicon, magnesium, phosphorous, zinc, potassium, nitrogen and sulphur
• Foods: lentils, buckwheat, alfalfa, whole rice, brewers yeast, sprouted grains, beetroot, rye, sardines, liquid chlorophyll, omega 3 oil and lots of fresh vegetables

Juices to help: • Grape • Blackberry • Watercress • Parsley

Nervous System

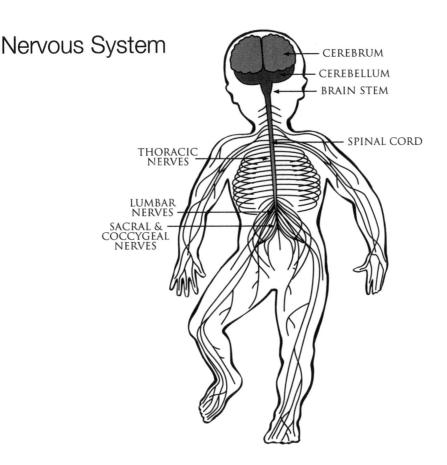

CEREBRUM
CEREBELLUM
BRAIN STEM
SPINAL CORD
THORACIC NERVES
LUMBAR NERVES
SACRAL & COCCYGEAL NERVES

The central nervous system consists of the brain, spinal cord and the body's extensive nerve network.

The brain is linked to the spinal cord, which is a column of nerves and tissue and extends two thirds of the way down the backbone. The nerves, which are attached to the spinal cord, spread throughout the body and carry impulses to and from the brain. The peripheral nervous system includes the autonomic nervous system, which is involved in the 'fight or flight' and 'negative' responses.

The human brain is much more complex than any computer and contains the thalamus, which relays all sensory nerve impulses, except the sense of smell. The olfactory bulb receives smells and sends them to the brain.

The hypothalamus has much to do with body temperatures, blood pressure, hunger, thirst, fear and anger.

The brain stem is a bundle of nerves which play a part in the function of the heart, lungs and digestive system.

Specific nutrients needed to nourish this system
• Vitamins: A, B, C, D, E, F, folic acid and niacin B vitamins in whole grains (plus oats, rice and wheat germ), wild blue-green algae and cabbage, really strengthen the nerves
• Minerals: calcium, phosphorous, magnesium, iron, sulphur, iodine, potassium and zinc magnesium foods help to calm the nerves, as does dill, basil and chamomile tea, while calcium helps them to function in the body
• Foods: fish, raw goats milk, egg yolk, nutritional yeast, chicken, meat and dairy (if tolerated)

Juices to help:
• Prune • • Carrot • Almond milk
• Celery

Skeletal System

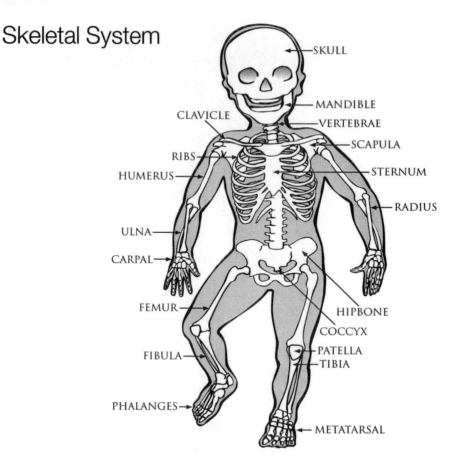

SKULL

MANDIBLE

CLAVICLE

VERTEBRAE

SCAPULA

RIBS

STERNUM

HUMERUS

RADIUS

ULNA

CARPAL

FEMUR

HIPBONE

COCCYX

PATELLA

FIBULA

TIBIA

PHALANGES

METATARSAL

The skeleton comprises more than 260 bones, formed from cartilage which changes to bone before our birth. These bones are more than the framework that shapes us. Apart from being a support for our muscles and ligaments (which, by contraction, allow us to move), bones are the storehouse of a jelly-like substance called red bone marrow, which produces millions of red blood cells (approx. every 120 days) to replace the old worn out cells that have done their work. Our entire blood supply system is replaced every 21 days. These new cells carry oxygen from the lungs to the body tissue.

Some of the vital organs of the body are protected by the very strong bones i.e. the brain by the skull and the heart and lungs by the rib cage.
As the bones are formed from calcium, phosphorous, vitamin D, other minerals and a protein called collagen, we need to make sure we supply our body with these nutrients.

Specific nutrients needed to nourish this system :
• Vitamins: approx. 20 minutes per day of sunshine (vitamin D) with maximum body trunk exposure
• Minerals: Calcium, Zinc, Iron, Potassium, Magnesium & Sodium
• Foods: grains, almonds, lots of yellow vegetables and some good quality dairy and meats (not much sugar as sweet foods retard calcium metabolism)

Juices to help:
• Raw goat's milk • Black 4 • Celery
• Parsley

Muscular System

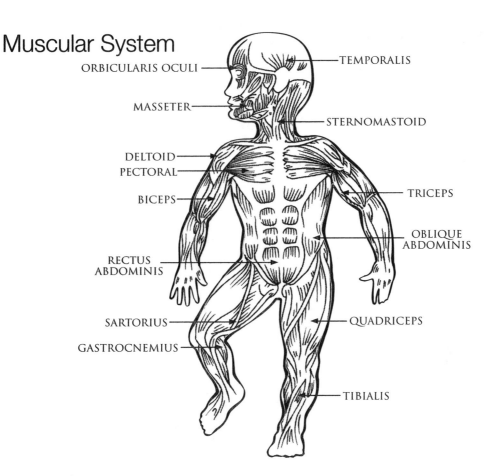

ORBICULARIS OCULI

TEMPORALIS

MASSETER

STERNOMASTOID

DELTOID
PECTORAL

BICEPS

TRICEPS

OBLIQUE
ABDOMINIS

RECTUS
ABDOMINIS

SARTORIUS

QUADRICEPS

GASTROCNEMIUS

TIBIALIS

There are approximately 650 muscles in the body and there are three quite different types.

The skeleton muscles move the arms, legs and spine by contraction. These muscles are connected to the skeleton bones by ligaments or tendons and respond to messages sent from the brain.

The visceral muscles control the movement of the blood through the hollow organs of the body i.e. the stomach, intestines and eyes. These muscles respond to the autonomic nervous system; for example, the muscle moves the food down the throat when we need to swallow.

The cardiac muscle is found only in the heart and its contraction movement is produced by nerve impulses sent from a small piece of tissue called a pacemaker.

All muscles need to be exercised; the skeletal muscles by physical exercise, the visceral muscles by chewing our food well and eating the right foods, while the cardiac muscle can be strengthened by eating grains (particularly oats).

Specific nutrients needed to nourish this system:
• Vitamins: A, B complex, C, D, E, biotin, choline and pantothenic acid
• Minerals: calcium, potassium, magnesium, silicon, nitrogen and iron
• Foods: all grains, lima beans, sprouts and fish (NB: too much protein causes loss of calcium by way of urine)

Juices to help: • Nut milks • Chlorophyll

Immune or Lymphatic System

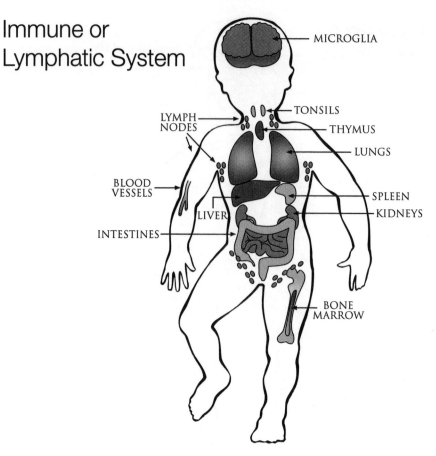

MICROGLIA

TONSILS

LYMPH NODES

THYMUS

LUNGS

BLOOD VESSELS

SPLEEN

KIDNEYS

LIVER

INTESTINES

BONE MARROW

The lymphatic system is a second type of circulation, which intertwines with the blood vessels. The spleen (part of the system) also removes used red blood cells from the body. Adenoids and tonsils are made of lymphatic tissue and act as barriers to bacteria and viruses.

Lymph nodes are small lumpy structures scattered through the body, with the neck, armpits and groin having the greatest numbers. Lymph nodes act as a trap for bacteria and contain white blood cells which attack foreign matter and stop infection through the production of antibodies.

The watery fluid which makes up our lymph system contain substances that the body uses to fight infection. The lymphatic system fluid flows backwards through the network of nodes by the action of valves, and the two main branches of the system join the veins at the base of the neck and become incorporated in the blood stream.

Specific nutrients needed to nourish this system
• Vitamins: A, all Bs, C, biotin, folic acid, choline and pantothenic acid
• Minerals: potassium and sodium
• Foods: green leafy vegetables, apple, celery and watercress

Juices to help: • Celery • Parsley • Carrot • Apple

Endocrine System

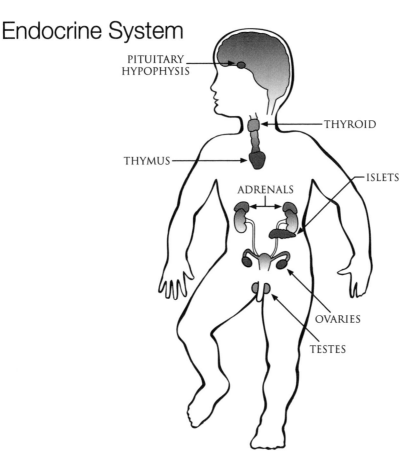

PITUITARY
HYPOPHYSIS

THYROID

THYMUS

ISLETS

ADRENALS

OVARIES

TESTES

Although the size of a pea, the pituitary is the master gland of the body. It is located in the skull about level with the top of the nose and is connected to the part of the brain which controls the hormone output of the pituitary.

This hormone in turn, stimulates all other endocrine glands. Various functions and rhythms of the body are controlled by hormones, which are chemical messages produced by the endocrine glands. These glands include the pituitary, thyroid, parathyroids, thymus, adrenals, Islets of Langerhans and the sex glands or gonads. Hormones are responsible for the rapid growth of a baby, the slower rate of growth through childhood and then the burst of growth during adolescence.

· The thyroid controls the rate of chemical processes in the body.
· The parathyroid controls the level of calcium in the blood.
· The thymus controls a type of white cell used to fight infection in children.
· Adrenals control salt and water balance in the body and help prepare the body to cope with emergencies.
· Islets of Langerhans in the pancreas control the level of sugar in the blood.

Specific nutrients needed to nourish this system :
• Vitamins: B complex, C, E, inositol, folic acid and pantothenic acid
• Minerals: iodine, silicon, phosphorous, calcium, magnesium, sodium, iron & potassium
• Foods: lecithin, sea-vegetables, green vegetables, eggs, seeds & nuts

Juices to help: • Pineapple • Black cherry
• Chlorophyll (green juice)

Integument System
(Skin)

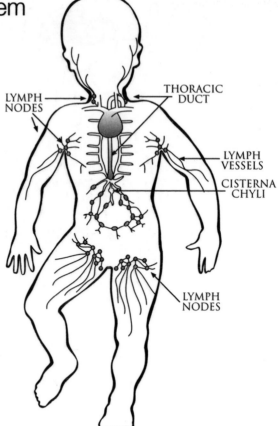

LYMPH
NODES

THORACIC
DUCT

LYMPH
VESSELS

CISTERNA
CHYLI

LYMPH
NODES

The integument system consists of the skin, hair, nails, oil and sweat glands, immune cells and antibodies and some glands.

The lymphatic system also plays a part in this system by producing immune cells. It also helps regulate body temperature (sweat glands) and alerts us to pain or pressure.

Skin is dry and slightly acid and because it is constantly being replaced by new cells, it is hard for bacteria to enter the body except where the skin is broken.

Specific nutrients needed to nourish this system :
• Vitamins: A, B complex, C, D, E, F, K, pantothenic acid, folic acid, niacin and bioflavonoid
• Minerals: silicon, calcium, fluorine, iron, sulphur, iodine, copper, manganese, zinc and magnesium
• Foods: rice, sea vegetables, whey, millet, sprouts, avocado, apple, cucumber, sea fish
and raw goat's milk

Urinary System

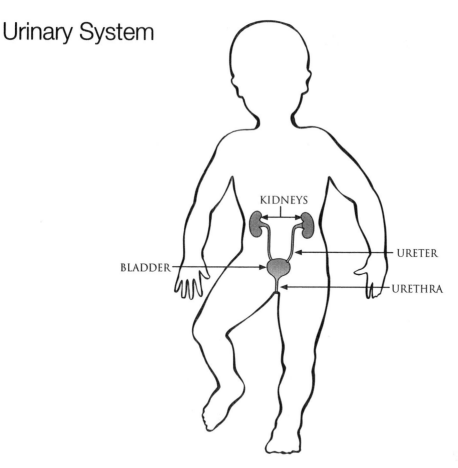

KIDNEYS

BLADDER

URETER

URETHRA

The urinary system consists of the kidneys, ureters, bladder and urethra. The blood filters through the kidneys, which release excess water and waste products as urine. The urine travels down the ureters to be stored in the bladder and then discharged from the body through the urethra.

The urinary system is also responsible for maintaining the acid/alkaline balance in the body; it regulates chemical composition of the blood and electrolyte balance.

Specific nutrients needed to nourish this system:
• Vitamins: A, B complex, C, D, E, and pantothenic acid
• Minerals: calcium, potassium, manganese, silicon, iron and magnesium
• Foods: liquid chlorophyll, green leafy vegetables, parsley, asparagus, apple and watermelon

Juices to help: • Celery • Blackcurrant • Grape • Parsley

Excretory System

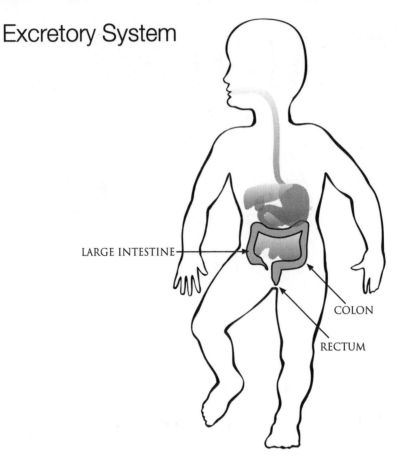

LARGE INTESTINE

COLON

RECTUM

The bowel or colon is a 1.4 metre long tube in an adult. Its function is to absorb water and the remaining nutrients from food that have been processed through the body, and to pass the remaining residue out through the rectum.

To keep the colon healthy we need grain fibre in our food, a reasonable amount of fluid, some exercise and lots and lots of vegetables.

Specific nutrients needed to nourish this system :
• Vitamins: A, all Bs, E, folic acid and niacin
• Minerals: magnesium, sulphur, calcium, iron and sodium
• Foods: green leafy vegetables (chlorophyll), yoghurt and all soured milk products, well cooked grains, flaxseed, sprouted seeds and all types of squash

Juices to help: • Black cherry • Celery • Parsley • Chlorophyll

Reproductive system

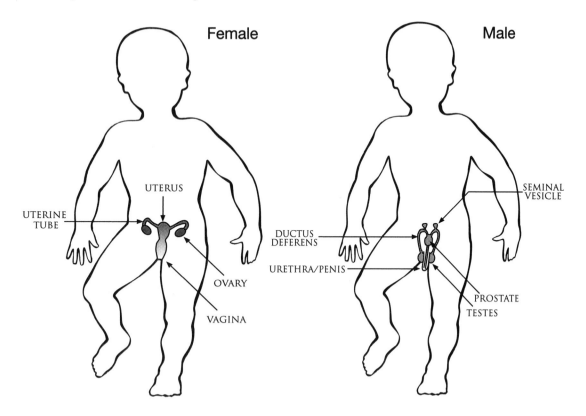

Female

UTERUS

UTERINE
TUBE

OVARY

VAGINA

Male

SEMINAL
VESICLE

DUCTUS
DEFERENS

URETHRA/PENIS

PROSTATE
TESTES

The female reproductive system is concerned with the secretion of sex hormones, and the production and transportation of gene cells.

The sex glands are the ovaries: an egg, or ovum, forms in one of the ovaries and travels along the Fallopian Tube to enter the womb. If it is fertilized it attaches to the wall of the womb. If not fertilized, the lining of the womb and the egg are discarded by the body approximately every 28 days.

All these activities and the making of hormones are controlled by the pituitary gland in the brain.

The male reproductive system or organs are the testicles, seminal vesicles or prostate glands. They not only produce sperm, but the male sex hormones. These hormones pass into the blood stream and give the male a deep voice and facial hair. Sperm are stored in the epididymes and travel along ducts through various glands to form semen.

Specific nutrients needed to nourish this system :
• Vitamins: A, B complex, C, D, E and F
• Minerals: Zinc, calcium, iodine, phosphorous, iron, sodium, potassium and silicon
• Foods: All seeds (including pumpkin and sesame and nut butters), egg yolk, lecithin and raw goat's milk.

RECIPES

Many childhood problems can be traced back to their food and particularly to wheat, dairy, egg, sugar and fats. The following recipes are free of many of these substances. Initially taking the time to check your choice of food against the nutrients charts will allow you to feel confident in providing appropriate quantities of protein, calcium and iron, for your child. Providing a wide range of well grown vegetables, fruit and grains, minimising the intake of preservative filled packaged foods will balance the sugar and fats in your meals.

The majority of these recipes are suitable for the whole family. They are in quantities for approximately 4 people. The nutrient content has been divided in 4 to give the amount of nutrients for 1 person. For a smaller child, divide again.

If dealing with a specific problem and needing to find more nutrients for a particular condition refer to the body system associated with the problem and add those foods that would be beneficial. Refer to the nutrient chart and gauge how much of those foods will be required to help the situation.

Example; for respiratory problems or even a cold, leave out or at least cut down the amount of dairy in the diet and increase the foods containing Vitamin C and immune boosting foods.

Complementary or natural therapies can help a great deal with the many health problems children present to us. The protein, calcium and iron content of the recipes are the most asked for quantities by parents of small children.

Change eating habits. Teach children to sit down and chew their food, even snacks, preferably not in front of the television. Sit with them at meal times to show a good example.

These recipes do not generally include the nutrients in the seasonings. These can vary greatly depending on the product and on personal choice of seasoning. There is an approximate nutrient content on page 35 - 40. Parsley and yeast flakes added to your food can make a big difference to the nutrient content. So remember these when deciding on your meals.

Most recipes are without fat.
If there is any fat in a recipe it is noted.

Cakes and desserts
These items vary greatly in portion consumed and are better eaten only occasionally. Children quickly develop a taste for sugar as it is satisfying for the moment but can become a major contribution to obesity even at a very early age.

VEGETABLE RECIPES

ASPARAGUS ROLLS

Serves 4

*1 425 g can asparagus spears
(approx. 20-22 spears)
Required amount of sliced whole wheat bread
(20 slices)
1 105 g can salmon or tuna
Soy mayonnaise or spread of choice*

Drain asparagus and fish.
Mash fish with mayonnaise.
Cut the crusts from the bread slices and roll
each slice with a rolling pin to make thin and
easier to spread with the mayonnaise and fish.
Lay 1 asparagus spear diagonally across the
slice and roll up firmly.
Secure with a toothpick.
Can be served as is or in layers in a casserole
dish. Cover and heat in the oven.
If hot, serve with a cheese sauce and a sprinkle
of parsley.
Allow 4-5 rolls per person.
A good lunch dish.
For main meal serve with salad.

	Per Serve
Protein	34 g
Calcium	273 mg
Iron	0.29 mg

Dairy and Egg Free

CAULIFLOWER CREPES

Serves 4

Crepe Batter:
*1 cup wholemeal plain flour
1 egg (optional)
½ tsp Herbamare or vegie salt
1 tsp salt skip raising agent
Equal parts soy milk and water. (Difficult to
be exact with amount, depends on dryness of
the flour, enough to mix flour and egg to a thin
cream consistency). Should make 8 crepes.*

Preheat crepe or stainless steel frying pan.
Lightly grease with unsalted butter.
Pour batter to form a 15cm circle into the pan.
Cook until small bubbles rise.
Turn over and cook other side. Keep warm.

Cauliflower Sauce:
*1 cup steamed cauliflower per person
2 tbs chopped spring onions
½ cup mustard sauce for each person
½ tsp herbamare salt*

Mustard Sauce:
*2 cups water
2 cups soy milk
½ tsp hot mustard
2 tbs soy mayonnaise
2 tbs cornflour mixed with ½ cup cold water*

Heat milk and water and mustard to boiling
point, thicken with kuzu or cornflour, boil for 1
minute. Whisk through soy mayonnaise. Heat
½ the sauce and add to cauliflower, onions, salt
and parsley - divide mixture into 8 and fill and
roll crepes. Heat other ½ of the sauce,
pour over rolled crepes.

	Per Serve
Protein	9 g
Calcium	47 mg
Iron	2 mg

59

CHEEZEY VEGETABLE FRITTERS

Makes 10

2 cups grated zucchini
¾ cup grated carrot
¾ cup grated cheese
4 spring onions, sliced finely
1 tsp herbamare or soy sauce
1 tsp dill seed or mixed herbs
¾ cup plain flour of choice
2 eggs
Optional – tomato sauce or plain yoghurt for
serving

Squeeze as much liquid as possible (with your
hand) from the zucchini and carrot.
Place in a bowl with next 5 ingredients and
mix well. Add the eggs and mix again.
Heat a skillet or frying pan, lightly grease with
unsalted butter or a smear of olive oil.
Place tablespoons of mix in the pan, flatten to
7 cm rounds, cook 3-4 minutes before turning
and cooking a further 5 minutes on the other
side. Serve with tomato sauce or plain yoghurt.

	Per Serve
Protein	2 g
Calcium	49 mg
Iron	0.5 mg
Saturated Fat	1.5 g

Wheat and Dairy Free

CORN STUFFED TOMATOES

Serves 4

4 medium tomatoes
½ cup chopped onions
2 cups corn kernels
½ cup mashed tofu
1 dsp miso
½ tsp basil
2 tbs chopped parsley
¾ cup fresh breadcrumbs (rye or spelt)
1 tsp crushed garlic

Cut a thin slice off the top of each tomato.
Scoop out pulp.
Saute the onions in 1 tbs water.
Place ½ cup of the corn in a blender along
with tofu and miso.
Blend until smooth and creamy.
If the mixture is too thick to blend add 1 tbs
of water.
In a bowl, combine the creamed mixture with
the sauted onions, the remaining corn, parsley
and basil. Mix well.
Fill the tomato shells with this mixture.
Mix breadcrumbs and garlic, sprinkle over
stuffed tomatoes.
Can be served cold immediately or place on
greased tray and bake in oven at 180° for 25
- 30 minutes.

	Per Serve
Protein	8 g
Calcium	30 mg
Iron	1 mg

Wheat, Dairy and Egg Free

CREAMED BRUSSEL SPROUTS

Serves 4

4 cups quartered brussel sprouts
1 cup yoghurt
1 cup sliced capsicums
1 cup sliced onions

Steam sprouts for 15 minutes.
Add capsicums and onions and steam another
5 minutes. Stir yoghurt through.

	Per Serve
Protein	21 g
Calcium	78 mg
Iron	2 mg
Saturated Fat	2.5 g

Wheat and Egg Free

CREAMY CORN & RED PEPPER CHOWDER

Serves 4

1 cup tofu
6 cups water
2 tbs arrowroot powder
1 tbs onion powder
1 cup diced red capsicum
2 garlic cloves
½ tsp dried thyme
½ cup water, extra
1 tbs mineral bouillon
1 cup diced onion
½ tsp sea salt
2 cups corn kernels

Place 1 cup of water and tofu into a blender
and puree.
Add the arrowroot, onion powder, garlic and
thyme and process for a few minutes.
Place diced onion in a pan and add the
remaining water.
Cook for a few minutes, add red capsicum,
corn kernels salt and bouillon.
Simmer for 10 minutes, stir in tofu mix, reheat
and add extra water if chowder is too thick.

	Per Serve
Protein	12 g
Calcium	51 mg
Iron	2 mg

Wheat, Dairy and Egg Free

CREPE STACKS

Serves 2-4

1¼ cups wholemeal flour (or spelt or half
wholemeal/half other)
1 egg
¼ tsp Herbamare or vegetable salt
2 tsp baking powder substitute or
1 tsp baking powder
½-¾ cup soy milk and water (equal parts) or
undiluted oat milk or cows milk

Sift dry ingredients into a bowl.
Break egg into the milk mix, beat gently.
Make a small well in the flour mix.
Pour in the liquid and slowly incorporate
the flour into the liquid and mix to a cream-
consistency batter.
You may need to add a little more liquid,
depending on the dryness of your flour.

Preheat crepe pan or stainless steel frying pan.
Lightly grease with a little unsalted butter.
Pour enough batter into the pan to thinly
cover the base.
Tilting the pan to extend batter to the edge
of pan, allow to cook until small bubbles rise
– about 30-40 seconds. Turn over and cook for
a further 15 seconds. Repeat process to make
6 crepes. Keep warm.

Filling:

4 cups diced sweet potato
6 cups shredded silver beet, spinach
or Asian greens
6 cups sliced mushrooms
tamari

Steam sweet potato and silver beet separately.
Saute mushrooms in a little tamari and water.
Mash sweet potato roughly.
Drain excess liquid from mushrooms and silver
beet. Keep warm. Divide each of the fillings
into two. Place one crepe on a plate, cover
with silver beet.

Top with another crepe, cover with the sweet
potato. Top with another crepe and then the
mushrooms.
Repeat using the other 3 crepes.
Cut into 4 to serve adding a sauce of your
choice.
Cheese flavoured white sauce is good.

	Per Serve
Protein	144 g
Calcium	151 mg
Iron	4.5 mg
Saturated Fat	1 g

HOT NOODLES AND VEGETABLES

Serves 4

1 cup carrots finely sliced
1 cup snow peas finely sliced
1 cup spring onion finely sliced
1 cup red capsicum finely sliced
1 cup cabbage finely sliced
2 tbs grated green ginger
1 tsp crushed garlic
2 tbs tamari or soy sauce
1 cup almonds
1 x 250 g packet rice pasta spirals
Parsley

Boil pasta according to directions on packet.
Steam or par boil carrots, cabbage, capsicum,
snow peas and spring onions.
Add ginger, garlic, soy sauce and almonds.
Stir through pasta, top with parsley.

	Per Serve
Protein	14 g
Calcium	140 mg
Iron	3 mg

Wheat, Dairy and Egg Free

CURRIED CAULIFLOWER WITH PASTA

Serves 4

2 onions
1 red capsicum (cut into small strips)
2 tsp cumin seeds
3 tsp curry powder
2 tbs rice flour
3 cups soy milk (½ and ½ water)
Medium cauliflower, chopped and steamed
1 cup almonds, chopped

Saute onions in water until soft.
Add red capsicum, cumin seeds, curry powder and rice flour.
Cook for 2-3 minutes.
Gradually stirring in soy milk and water.
Stir until boiling and thickened.
Mix steamed cauliflower into sauce carefully.
When serving sprinkle with chopped almonds.

Pasta:
Cook pasta of choice according to packet instructions.

	Per Serve
Protein	4.5 g
Calcium	40 mg
Iron	1.5 mg

Dairy and Egg Free
Wheat Free (if using rice pasta)

GLUTEN FREE CREPES

2 cups gluten free flour (eg. ¾ cup rice flour,
¾ cup potato flour, ½ cup soy flour)
2 eggs
¾ cup water
For savoury crepes add herbs and vegetable salt etc
For sweet crepes add spices, honey, vanilla.

Sift flours, beat in eggs and water.
Stand for ½ hour.
Pour approx 2 tbs into lightly greased crepe pan and cook over medium heat for a minute or so.
Flip and cook other side.
Can be used as roll ups, wraps, a base or as dessert.

Sauce:

1 cup orange juice
¾ cup lemon juice
½ cup chopped dates
¼ cup cornflour or arrowroot

Place all ingredients in a saucepan over heat and stir until thickening is dissolved.
Bring to the boil and boil 1 minute.
Can be used as sauce over crepes or over any cake or dessert.

	Per Serve
Protein	37 g
Calcium	188 mg
Iron	6.5 mg

Wheat and Dairy Free

LASAGNE

Serves 4

10-12 sheets instant corn lasagne noodles
2 bunches spinach
4 cups grated pumpkin
4 chopped onions

Sauce:
1 400 g can chopped tomatoes
3 tomatoes
1 small onion
1 tsp each basil, oregano, sage and garlic
½ tsp salt Herbamare or sea salt

Preheat oven to 200° C for lasagne.

Sauce Method:
Chop tomatoes and onion.
Place in a saucepan with the rest of the sauce ingredients. Simmer for 15 minutes.
When cooked, mash well or puree.

Lasagne:
While sauce is cooking wash and chop roughly, then steam spinach.
Peel and slice onion thinly and steam it and the pumpkin.
Grease casserole dish with unsalted butter.
Spoon a thin layer of tomato sauce into the base of the casserole dish, cover with sheets of lasagne noodles breaking noodles to fit dish, if necessary.
Layer spinach/onion, pumpkin, spinach/onion, pumpkin with noodles and sauce in between each layer. Cover dish and cook for ¾ hour at 200°C. Can sprinkle with parmesan and parsley before serving.

	Per Serve
Protein	5.2 g
Calcium	172 mg
Iron	2 mg

Wheat, Dairy and Egg Free

LEMON BAKED VEG

Serves 4

2 large brown onions
1 medium sweet potato cut into chunky pieces
4 small potatoes cut in quarters
2 parsnips cut into chunky pieces
2 medium lemons
8 small carrots cut into chunky pieces
4 unpeeled cloves garlic
6 sprigs fresh rosemary

Cut onions and lemons into eight wedges.
Place onion, lemon, carrot, potatoes, sweet potatoes, parsnips garlic and rosemary in a baking dish.
Bake covered for about ¾ hour or until tender.
Remove cover. Increase oven temperature to hot. Turn over the vegetables.
Bake about 20 minutes or until brown.
Serve with green leafy vegetables and a cooked grain.

	Per Serve
Protein	6 g
Calcium	106 mg
Iron	2.5 mg

POTATO CHIPS

Potatoes
Scrub required amount of potatoes.
Cut into fat wedges.
Place skin side down on a greased tray.
Cover with another tray or greased greaseproof paper.
Put in moderate oven.
Let steam until nearly cooked.
Turn over the chips.
Remove cover and increase oven heat to allow wedges to crisp and brown.
Sprinkle with Herbamare if liked.

POTATO BAKE

300 g cooked mashed potatoes
4 large eggs beaten
1 onion chopped finely
½ cup chopped parsley
½ tsp salt or vegetable seasoning

Saute the onion in a little water, mix all
ingredients together.
Put 1 tablespoon of oil in a pan,
tilt to grease sides of pan.
Heat pan and pour in the mix.
Heat gently until bottom is browned and then
place the pan under a hot griller
to brown the top.
Cut in slices and serve with vegetables or salad,
hot or cold.

	Per Serve
Protein	28 g
Calcium	146 mg
Iron	7.5 mg

POTATO CAKES

Potatoes
Egg white and 2 tbs water
Crumbs – wholemeal bread, spelt bread, corn
crisp bread (crushed), rice flour, sesame seeds

Scrub required amount of potatoes.
Cut into 1 cm thick slices.
Steam for 5 minutes.
Beat 1 egg white with 2 tbs water.
Dip slices in mixture and then coat in the
crumbs of your choice.
Place on a greased oven tray and bake in a hot
oven for 10 – 15 minutes until nicely browned.

POTATO & CORN BAKE

Serves 4

4 cups scrubbed potatoes chopped
into 10 cm squares
½ cup spring onions
2 stalks celery, chopped
1 cup peas or diced beans
2 cups corn kernels
1 tsp paprika
3 cups mustard or white sauce
½ cup freshly chopped parsley

Steam potatoes and peas or beans until tender.
Mix in all the other ingredients except paprika
and sauce. Place in a greased casserole dish.
Top with sauce and paprika.
Bake in oven at 200°C for 30 minutes until
golden brown. Serve with chopped parsley.

Mustard Sauce:

1 cup soy milk
½ cup soy mayonnaise
2 tsp popped mustard seeds
1 tsp hot mustard
2 tbs chopped fresh chives or spring onion.

Mix all ingredients together well.

	Per Serve
Protein	10 g
Calcium	40 mg
Iron	2.5 mg
Saturated Fat	1 g

Wheat, Dairy and Egg Free

PUMPKIN & POTATO CASSEROLE

Serves 4

Casserole:

4 cups each thinly sliced potato and pumpkin

In a lightly greased casserole dish, place a little sauce, then alternate layers of potato and pumpkin (sprinkling the pumpkin lightly with Herbamare), finishing with pumpkin.
Pour remainder of sauce over vegetables.
Cover casserole dish with a lid and bake in a moderate oven for about 45 minutes or until vegetables are tender.

White Sauce:

2 cups soy milk
1 cup water
1 large onion - diced
1 bay leaf
2 tsp hot English mustard
½ tsp Herbamare – to taste
2 dsp corn flour
(mixed to a thin cream with cold water)

Boil the onion in water.
When transparent, add soy milk, Herbamare, bay leaf and mustard.
Bring back to boil, thicken with corn flour mix and let boil again for one minute.

	Per Serve
Protein	10 g
Calcium	98 mg
Iron	3 mg

Wheat, Dairy and Egg Free

PUMPKIN PATTIES

Serves 4

2 cups soaked, cooked, dried beans
of choice (1 cup raw)
2 cups mashed pumpkin
1 egg
1 tsp cumin
1 cup grated carrots
4 green   , chopped
1 cup breadcrumbs
½ tsp Herbamare seasoning

Blend or puree beans, stir in pumpkin.
Add egg, stir in carrots, shallots, cumin and Herbamare.

Divide into 8 portions, roll in breadcrumbs, place on a greased oven tray and dry bake in oven at 200°C for 20 minutes, turning once.

	Per Serve
Protein	8 g
Calcium	90 mg
Iron	3.5 mg

Dairy Free

RICE PAPER SALAD ROLLS

Serves 4

12 sheets rice paper approx 20 cm diameter
6 cups shredded cabbage, red or green
1 cup chopped fresh mint
½ cup fat free French dressing
4 cups shredded lettuce
2 cups julienned red capsicum
2 cups sliced snow peas
1 punnet alfalfa sprouts
150 gr tofu, cut in 12 strips, marinate in ½ cup
tamari and ½ cup water for 30 minutes

Lightly steam cabbage, rinse and cool and add
dressing and mint.
Soak rice paper sheets, one at a time in a bowl
of warm water until soft and pliable.
Lay on a clean tea towel; layer 1/12th of
ingredients in the centre of the rice sheet.
Roll up, tucking in the ends as you roll.
Serve with a dipping sauce of choice.
Fillings can be varied to suit taste.
Lettuce leaves can also be used this way. Just
wash and lay one or two leaves flat and put
fillings in the centre and roll up.

	Per Serve
Protein	9 g
Calcium	147 mg
Iron	16 mg

Wheat, Dairy and Egg free

ROSTI

Serves 4 – 6

1½ kg potatoes
2 tbs butter
4 tbs olive oil
2 tbs spring onion , chopped
½ tsp sea salt

Scrub, then boil the potatoes in their skins.
Allow them to cool thoroughly, peel and grate
coarsely.
Melt the butter and oil in a large pan and add
potatoes which have been mixed with salt and
onion.
Cook on a low to medium heat until
underneath is browned (lift one side to check),
slide onto a greased plate and return to pan
upside down to cook and brown on the other
side. Cut into wedges to serve.

	Per Serve
Protein	14 g
Calcium	26 mg
Iron	2 mg

SAUERKRAUT

Serves 2-4

2 cups chopped red cabbage
1 cup chopped green cabbage
1 clove garlic chopped
2 tsp honey
1 tbs chopped red onion
1 tsp dill seeds or tips
1 tbs apple cider vinegar
1 cup water

Combine cabbages, garlic, onion, dill seeds and
water. Cook gently for a few minutes.
Add apple cider vinegar and honey, cook until
cabbage is soft. Can be served hot or cold.

	Per Serve
Protein	4.5 g
Calcium	51 mg
Iron	7 mg

Wheat Egg and Dairy free

SAUSAGE ROLL SUBSTITUTES

Serves 4

2 sheets reduced fat puff pastry
1 x 400 g can chick peas
100 g plain tofu
¾ cup chopped sun dried tomatoes
¾ cup chopped spring onions
1 tsp cumin powder
2 tbs basil pesto
1 tbs lemon juice
1 tbs tamari or soy sauce
1 egg (optional)

With a rolling pin and on a floured surface, roll pastry sheets thinner.
Cut each sheet horizontally into three strips.
Mash chick peas and tofu, combine with other ingredients. Divide mixture into 6 portions.
Place a portion onto centre of each strip lengthways.
Wet the top edge of strip and roll up.
Cut each roll into 6, place on a greased oven slide, brush with water or melted butter.
Sprinkle with dill and sesame seeds and bake at 200°C for 30 minutes or until golden brown.
Can add a 210 g tin of salmon or tuna to the basic mix.

	Per Serve
Protein	25 g
Calcium	187 mg
Iron	6.5 mg

SAVOURY CORN LOAF

2 cups polenta or 1 1/2 cups polenta and 1/2 cup spelt flour
3 tsp aluminium free baking powder
1 egg
1 cup oat or soy milk
1 tbs olive oil
1 tbs gherkin spread or relish

2 tbs chopped sundried tomatoes

Mix dry ingredients together.
Mix together all the remaining ingredients.
Add the two mixes together stirring only until combined, do not over-mix.
Place mixture in 20 cm greased loaf pan and bake at 200° for approximately 30 minutes.

Variation: omit savoury flavourings and add 2 tbs honey for a sweet loaf.

	Per Serve
Protein	39 g
Calcium	49 mg
Iron	9 mg

Wheat and Dairy free

SCALLOPED SWEET POTATOES

Serves 2-3

1 large sweet potato, unpeeled and sliced
2 large red onions thinly sliced
1 cup soy milk
1 clove garlic

Lay slices of sweet potato in greased baking dish.
Add sliced onion over potatoes.
Mix crushed garlic into soy milk.
Pour over potatoes.
Cover for first 30 minutes.
Cook in moderate oven 180°C for about ¾ hour. Remove cover and allow to brown.

	Per Serve
Protein	7 g
Calcium	105 mg
Iron	3 mg

SHASHLIK

Serves 4

½ block of tofu
½ block of tempeh
2 onions, cut into 8 pieces
1 capsicum, cut into 8 pieces
2 carrots, cut into 8 pieces
2 zucchini, cut into 8 pieces
8 small tomatoes
3 tbs tamari
3 tbs water
1 tsp grated green ginger
1 clove garlic
8 skewers

Cut tofu and tempeh into cubes and marinate in tamari, ginger and water.
Cut onions into wedges and carrots into thick slices.
Cut capsicums into large pieces.
Steam vegetables till almost cooked, cool under running cold water.
Thread vegetables, tofu and tempeh alternatively onto skewers.
Cook on hot plate on a BBQ or on a greased oven tray in the oven at 200°C for 15 minutes.

	Per Serve
Protein	16 g
Calcium	157 mg
Iron	3 mg

Wheat, Dairy and Egg Free

STUFFED CABBAGE LEAVES

Serves 4

8 large cabbage leaves
2 cups mashed tofu
1 cup grated carrot
1 cup grated zucchini
(squeeze out juice by hand)
1 cup chopped
4 tomatoes, chopped
½ tsp dill seeds
½ tsp dried basil
2 tsp tamari sauce
Stock or tomato juice, extra herbs or parmesan cheese

Steam cabbage leaves until pliable.
Combine all other ingredients except stock or juice, divide mixture into 8 and roll one portion up in each leaf, tucking in the ends.
Place in an ovenproof dish and cover with stock or tomato juice, sprinkle with herbs or parmesan cheese.
Bake at 200°C for 45 minutes.
Serve with brown rice or lentils and a green vegetable.

	Per Serve
Protein	8 g
Calcium	129 mg
Iron	3 mg
Saturated Fat	6 g

Wheat, Dairy and Egg Free

STUFFED POTATOES (1)

Serves 4

4 large potatoes
150 g tofu
2 spring onions, chopped
1 cup corn kernels
1 cup sweet potato, diced
1 tsp Herbamare
Optional – grated cheese to top

Scrub and prick potatoes.
Cook in oven , covered for first 30 minutes, uncovered for another 30 minutes, or steam whole. Cook and mash sweet potato.
Mash tofu.
Mix tofu, spring onion , sweet potato, corn and herbamare.
Cut top off potatoes, scoop out centre and mash in with tofu etc.
Pile back into potato shells, can top with grated cheese.
Return to oven 200°C to reheat for 15 – 20 minutes.

	Per Serve
Protein	8 g
Calcium	110 mg
Iron	3 mg

Wheat and Egg Free
Dairy Free (if not using cheese)

STUFFED POTATOES (2)

Serves 4

4 good sized potatoes
1 cup finely chopped onions
1 cup finely chopped mushrooms
1 cup cooked mashed sweet potato
½ tsp savoury or herb of choice
2 tbs barley or rice miso
2 tbs chopped parsley
pinch of sweet paprika

Scrub and bake the potatoes for 1 hour at 180° or until cooked.
Saute onion and mushrooms with herbs, set aside.
When potatoes are done, cut in half and scoop out the centre leaving 1 cm of potato in shell.
Mash potato and other vegetables together with seasoning.
Put back into shell and top with paprika.
Return to oven to reheat and brown on top.

	Per Serve
Protein	7 g
Calcium	52 mg
Iron	2 mg

Wheat, Dairy and Egg Free

STUFFED SQUASH

2 medium squash
½ cup fresh breadcrumbs
1 cup cooked brown rice
½ cup chopped celery
½ cup chopped carrots
¼ cup chopped parsley
¼ cup chopped spring onions
2 teaspoons mixed, chopped fresh herbs

Cut squash in half lengthwise.
Scoop out centre and fill with stuffing mix.
Press stuffing down well.
Cook for 20-30 minutes at 180°C until squash is soft.

	Per Serve
Protein	9 g
Calcium	72 mg
Iron	2 mg

Dairy and Egg Free

STUFFED TOMATOES

Serves 4

4 medium to large tomatoes
2 eggs
½ cup chopped spring onion
½ cup corn kernels
¼ tsp sea salt

Cut top off tomatoes and remove pulp carefully.
Scramble eggs with 1 tbs juice and pulp from the tomatoes and sea salt.
Stir in corn and spring onion and pile mixture back in to tomato shells.
Can be served cold or heated in the oven for 15-25 minutes.

	Per Serve
Protein	5.5 g
Calcium	25 mg
Iron	1 mg

Wheat and Dairy Free

SUMMER VEGETABLE MOULDS

Serves 4

2 very ripe tomatoes, chopped
2 cups tomato juice
3 tbs agar agar
1 chopped capsicum
2 cups tinned or cooked peas
1 cup corn kernels
1 tbs chopped parsley

Heat juice and add agar agar, stir constantly, bring to boil and simmer for 1 minute.
Cool a little, stir in the rest of the ingredients.
Pour into individual moulds and allow to set.
Turn out onto a bed of shredded lettuce and decorate with sliced tomato or avocado.

Sauce:

2 cups plain yoghurt
½ cups yeast flakes
1 tsp mustard
½ tsp herbamare

Blend all together. Serve over moulds.

	Per Serve
Protein	12 g
Calcium	213 mg
Iron	4.5 mg

Wheat and Egg Free
Dairy Free (if using soy yoghurt)

SWEET CORN PATTIES

Serves 4

1 cup buckwheat flour
1 cup rice flour
2 tsp curry powder
1 large onion
1½ cups corn
2 tbs chopped parsley
1 egg
1 tsp Herbamare
1½ cups milk (soy or oat)

Mix flours together. Beat egg and milk.
Mix all together.
Cook in spoonfuls on lightly greased grill or frypan.

	Per Serve
Protein	15 g
Calcium	45 mg
Iron	4 mg

Wheat Free
Dairy Free (if not using cows milk)

VEGETABLE AND CHICKPEA CURRY

Serves 4

2 tbs olive oil
2 tbs water
1 cup brown onion, thinly sliced
1 tbs grated fresh ginger
1 dsp garlic crushed
½ tsp dried turmeric
2 tsp ground coriander
2 tsp garam masala
2 potatoes, cut into 2" cubes
2 carrots, cut into 2" slices
2 zucchini, cut into 2" slices
2 cups chopped tomatoes
1½ cups reduced salt vegetable stock
or 3 stock cubes
400 g can chickpeas, rinsed and drained
2 cups baby spinach leaves, washed
1 cup fresh or frozen peas
1½ cups basmati rice
Papadums to serve

Heat oil in a large pot, add the onion and ginger and cook over a medium heat for 5 minutes or until soft.
Add the garlic and spices and cook for 2 minutes or until fragrant.
Add the potatoes and carrots and cook until the vegetables are coated in the spices.
Stir in the zucchini, tomatoes and stock and simmer.
Reduce heat and cook uncovered for 15 minutes or until the vegetables are tender and the curry has thickened slightly.
Add the chickpeas and stir.
Add spinach and peas; cook just until the spinach wilts and the peas are soft.
Cook the rice in boiling water over a high heat until tunnels appear in the rice.
Reduce heat to very low, cover and allow to steam for 10 minutes or until the rice is tender and all the liquid is absorbed.
Serve the curry on top of the rice and accompany with the papadums.

	Per Serve
Protein	30 g
Calcium	257 mg
Iron	10 mg

Wheat, Dairy and Egg Free

VEGETABLE BURGERS

4 cups grated vegetables of choice
¼ cup chopped spring onion
1 tbs mixed herbs
½ cup chopped parsley
1 cup crumbled tofu
2 tbs tamari
1 cup wholemeal bread crumbs
1 clove crushed garlic
1 egg or ½ cup wholemeal flour
A little water if needed to hold mix together

Steam vegetables lightly.
Mix all together in a bowl and divide into eight.
Shape each portion into a ball then flatten a little.
Coat in crumbs, bran or rice bran.
Place on a lightly greased tray and cook in a moderate oven for approximately 30 minutes, turning once - or fry in an electric fry pan if preferred.

VEGETABLE CHOICE PIE

Carrots
Diced pumpkin
Potatoes
Peas or corn
Soy sauce
Herbs of choice

Peel off thin strips of carrot with a vegetable
peeler and line a greased pie plate or individual
heatproof bowls with the carrot strips.
Fill plate or bowls with cooked (or tinned)
chick peas or beans, diced pumpkin, potatoes
and peas or corn. Sprinkle with soy sauce or
herbs of your choice, grate potato over the top
of vegetables and cook in a moderate oven
180°C for 45 minutes. Pies can be turned
upside down on a serving plate. Serve with
broccoli and green beans, brown rice or pasta.

Wheat, Dairy and Egg Free

VEGETABLE NUT LOAF

Serves 4

1 cup wholemeal or spelt fresh breadcrumbs
3 cups mixed vegetables (diced finely)
1 cup ground or chopped almonds
½ tsp sage
1 tsp Herbamare
2 eggs
1 cup milk of choice

Mix eggs and milk well.
Add to the rest of the ingredients.
Pack tightly into a greased loaf pan.
Bake in moderate oven 180° for 45 minutes.

	Per Serve
Protein	10.5 g
Calcium	258 mg
Iron	6 mg

VEGETABLE PATTIES

Serves 4

2 cups grated carrots
1 cup grated parsnips
1 cup grated turnips
½ cup grated swedes
1 cup grated potatoes
1 cup grated pumpkin
1-1 ½ tsp curry
2 tbs tamari
1 tsp cumin
¼ -½ cup rice flour
2 sliced stalks celery
1 clove crushed garlic
1 cup diced onions
1 egg
Herbamare to taste

Lightly steam all vegetables.
Mix all ingredients together.
Add enough flour to hold mix together.
Form into patties and bake on a lightly greased
oven tray (use unsalted butter) at 180° for
about 20 minutes or until golden brown,
turning once.

	Per Serve
Protein	5 g
Calcium	100 mg
Iron	2.5 mg

Wheat and Dairy Free

VEGETABLE SAUSAGES

2 cups cooked rice
2 cups cooked chickpeas pureed in blender or food processor
1 cup chopped onions
2 cups sweet potato
1 cup parsnip
½ – ¾ cup rice flour, enough to make a firm mix

Seasoning A
>2 tsp curry powder
>1 tsp coriander
>1 tsp cumin
>1 tbs tamari or Braggs
>Herbamare to taste
>1 – 2 tsp crushed garlic

Seasoning B
>cook extra 2 cups of onions and puree
>½ cup of tomato puree or
>1 cup of diced tomatoes
>2 tsp basil
>2 tsp mixed herbs

Lightly steam sweet potato, onions and parsnip then add to pureed chickpeas.
Once mixed all together add the rice flour and seasonings (A or B).
Pipe mixture through an icing bag without star nozzle in place.
Cut piped sausages into 12 – 15 cm lengths.
Roll in polenta or flour.
Place on greased tray and heat in oven 180°C for 15 minutes.

	Per Serve
Protein	82.5 g
Calcium	556 mg
Iron	23.5 mg

VEGETABLE STRUDEL

Serves 4

4 cups shredded cabbage
1 cup chopped zucchini
2 cups grated carrot
1 medium leek, sliced
1 tsp caraway seeds
1 tbs soy yoghurt mixed with 2 tbs mayonnaise
1 tbs rice flour
½ cup chopped chives
2 tsp French mustard
3 sheets of Filo pastry

Steam first 5 ingredients together, then cool.
Add the yoghurt/mayonnaise, chives, flour and mustard and mix through.
Place the 3 sheets of filo together and lay the filling along the centre lengthways.
Fold in the edges and roll the strudel up.
Brush with Soya milk and sprinkle with extra caraway seeds.
Bake in oven at 160°C for 35 minutes.

	Per Serve
Protein	3.9 g
Calcium	74 mg
Iron	2.5 mg

Egg Free

VEGETABLE SUSHI

Serves 4-8

8 toasted nori sheets
8 x 18 cm strips of carrot 6 mm (¼") thick
8 x 18 cm strips green capsicum
1½ cups chopped mushrooms
1 tsp horseradish cream
12 mm (½") piece chopped ginger root
2 cups brown rice
8 x 18 cm strips red capsicum
8 x 18 cm strips cucumber
2 cloves chopped garlic
¼ cup tamari
¼ cup apple cider vinegar and 1 tbs honey
mixed together

Cook brown rice until very soft, do not rinse
with water when cooked, just drain away any
excess water.
Stir in vinegar/honey mix.
Lightly steam carrots and capsicum.
Cook mushrooms in tamari, add garlic, drain
off any excess liquid, then puree mushrooms.
Puree ginger and horseradish, wash sugar off
if using preserved ginger.
Place sheets of nori on a flat surface, cover ¾
with sticky rice. Spread a thin layer of ginger
and horseradish, then layer of mushrooms, in a
strip across centre of rice followed by 1 strip
of each vegetable across nori rice sheet on top
of the mushrooms.
Wet a pastry brush with water and brush
along exposed top of nori sheet.
Roll up and seal. Refrigerate for 1 hour, cut
each roll into 6 portions.
Serve with tamari or soy sauce for dipping.

	Per Serve
Protein	15 g
Calcium	185 mg
Iron	3.5 mg

Wheat, Dairy and Egg Free

ZUCCHINI LOAF

Serves 4

2 cups cooked brown rice
2 cups broccoli flowerets
500 g zucchini – sliced
squeeze out excess moisture after steaming
raw zucchini to line tray
½ bunch chopped spring onions
½ cup ground almonds
2 tsp chopped garlic
2 tbs curry powder
½ cup soy flour
3 tbs tamari

Steam zucchini and broccoli.
Mix all other ingredients together then mix in
the zucchini and broccoli.
Line a greased tray with thin long strips of raw
zucchini, bottom and sides.
Spoon in the rice mixture, pat down well and
bake at 190°C for 35 minutes.
Allow to cool a little before turning out.

	Per Serve
Protein	30 g
Calcium	153 mg
Iron	3.5 mg

Wheat, Dairy and Egg Free

GRAIN & PULSE RECIPES

BAKED BEANS

Serves 4

2 cups beans of choice
(soaked overnight in cold water)

Sauce
4 medium tomatoes, chopped
2 diced onions
2 tbs chopped parsley
2 tsp basil
1 tsp Herbamare
½ cup water
2 cups seasoned bread crumbs of choice

Drain and cook beans until al dente
in fresh water.
Saute onions in ¼ cup of water, add tomatoes,
Herbamare and basil, add extra ¼ cup water,
cover and cook until tender.
Put cooked beans into a greased casserole or
baking dish.
Cover with the tomato sauce.
Sprinkle with breadcrumbs and bake
uncovered in oven at 180°C for 30-40 minutes.
Serve with chopped parsley.

	Per Serve
Protein	11 g
Calcium	55 mg
Iron	2.5 mg

Dairy and Egg Free
Gluten Free (if not using wheat bread)

BAKED EGG & BRAN PIE

Serves 4

2 tbs butter
2 medium zucchini thinly sliced
4 spring onions
1 cup chopped mushrooms
1 tsp thyme
1 tsp sage
6 eggs
¾ cup thin cream or milk of choice

Saute onions, mushrooms and zucchini in pan
with the melted butter.
Add seasonings.
Beat eggs and cream or milk together.
Place vegetables in a greased pie plate and
pour over egg mix.

Topping:
¾ cup oat bran
3 tbs grated hard cheese
3 tbs Parmesan cheese

Sprinkle topping over egg and vegetables.
Bake in moderated oven 180° for 45 minutes
or until set.

	Per Serve
Protein	10 g
Calcium	272 mg
Iron	7.5 mg

BAKED PUMPKIN AND TEMPEH RISOTTO

Serves 4

2 cups Arborio rice
3-4 vegetable cubes
2 tbs butter
3 cups jap or butternut pumpkin, peeled and finely diced
12 slices bacon or tempeh
½ cup finely grated Parmesan cheese
1 tbs chopped parsley
2 cups roughly chopped spinach

Preheat oven to 200°C.
Place rice, stock, butter and pumpkin in an ovenproof dish and cover tightly with lid or foil.
Bake for 30 minutes or until the rice is soft – the risotto may be quite liquid.
If you are using bacon, chop into small pieces and cook as desired. If using tempeh chop and grill.
After the 30 minutes, add the Parmesan, spinach, salt and parsley and stir for 2 minutes and serve.

	Per Serve
Protein	7 g
Calcium	118 mg
Iron	1 mg
Saturated Fat	5 gr

Wheat and Egg Free

BEAN DIP

2 cups cooked lima beans
2 tsp chopped garlic
2 tbs lemon juice
2 tbs soy yoghurt
½ tsp sweet paprika
1 tsp honey
2 tsp cumin
2 tbs cider vinegar

Puree beans in food processor.
Whiz in remaining ingredients.
Can be used as a dip or thinned down with water and used as a sauce on pasta or vegetables.

	Per Serve
Protein	26 g
Calcium	110 mg
Iron	5 mg

BEAN PATTIES

Serves 4

½ cup lentils
1 cup lima or canniloni beans
1 onions chopped
½ tsp garam masala
½ tsp ground cumin
pinch chilli powder
½ cup chopped tomatoes
1 cup rice
1 tbs chopped parsley
1 tsp miso

Soak beans overnight, cook, and mash.
Cook lentils and rice.
Puree rice.
Mix all ingredients together and shape into 8 patties. Place on a greased tray and bake in moderate oven for approximately ½ hour turning once.

	Per Serve
Protein	11 g
Calcium	36 mg
Iron	4 mg

Wheat, Dairy and Egg Free

CHICK PEA AND MUSHROOM CREAM SAUCE

Serves 4

500 g mushrooms, sliced
8 spring onions, chopped
3 tsp crushed garlic
½ cup water or stock
2 cups cooked chick peas
½ cup tamari
½ cup soy mayonnaise or sour cream
½ cup soy yoghurt
Cornflour to thicken – if needed

Saute mushrooms and garlic in 1 tbs water for 10 minutes.
Add chickpeas, spring onions and ½ cup water or stock.
Cook 10 minutes, thicken with cornflour if needed.
Add combined soy yoghurt and mayonnaise, season with tamari.
Serve with polenta triangles or over other grains or vegetables.

	Per Serve
Protein	23 g
Calcium	194 mg
Iron	12 mg
Saturated Fat	8 g

Wheat, Dairy and Egg Free

CHICK PEA & VEGIE ROLLS OR PARTY PIES

Makes 15-18

2 sheets shortcrust pastry, rolled to 30 cm long.
Cut into 4 strips or into rounds to fit into patty or muffin tins—line greased tins with round pastry bases.

3 cups cooked chick peas—roughly mashed
1 medium onion—chopped finely
1 cup each of chopped zucchini, celery and tomato
1 tsp chopped garlic
1 tsp Herbamare
2 tsp basil or mixed herbs of choice
½ cup chopped sun dried tomatoes
1 tbs soy mayonnaise
1 cup cooked brown rice
Optional extra:
1 small can of tuna or salmon

Lightly steam all vegetables, add seasonings and chick peas and mix well.
Fill patty tins and cover each pie with another round of pastry.
Brush tops with a little egg yolk or milk.
Cook for approximately 20 minutes at 200°C.
For vegetable rolls, lay filling along the centre of each strip of pastry.
Damp top edge of pastry with water and roll up.
Cut each roll into six and cook as for party pies.
Serve with your favourite dipping sauce.

	Per Serve
Protein	11.5 g
Calcium	83 mg
Iron	4 mg
Saturated Fat	2 g

Dairy and Egg Free

78

CHICK PEA LOAF

Serves 4

1 cup chick peas
(can use canned which will be 2 cups)
1 cup vegetable juice
(retained from cooked vegetables)
¾ cup chopped almonds
1 cup each celery, hulled millet and onion
2 tbs parsley
1 egg, optional
Herbamare

Soak chick peas overnight if using dried peas.
Strain off the soak water, add fresh water and
cook until soft.
Cook celery with millet and onion in 3 cups
water, strain, reserving 1 cup of liquid.
Mash chick peas with this cup of liquid and
season with Herbamare.
Mix peas, almonds and vegetables together, add
egg if required to bind, pack into a greased loaf
pan and bake at 160°C for 45 minutes.

	Per Serve
Protein	25 g
Calcium	146 mg
Iron	8 mg

Wheat & Dairy Free

DHAL

Serves 4

2 chopped onions
2 tsp crushed garlic
1 tsp coriander
1 tsp curry powder
½ tsp turmeric
2 cups red lentils
4 cups water
1 tsp Herbamare
1 tbs bouillon

Wash lentils well.
Saute onions and herbs in a little water.
Add the other ingredients and simmer for
about 1 hour, stirring occasionally.
Should be the consistency of a thick pea soup.

	Per Serve
Protein	39 g
Calcium	128 mg
Iron	10 mg

Wheat, Dairy and Egg Free

FALAFEL

Serves 4

2 cups dried chick peas
1 cup finely grated carrots
½ cup cooked rice
½ cup finely chopped chives or onions
2 crushed garlic cloves
¼ cup finely chopped parsley
1 tbs cumin
1 tsp garam masala
¼ tsp paprika
1 tsp cider vinegar
1 tsp coriander
2 tbs tamari

Soak peas overnight.
Throw away soak water, cover with fresh water
and cook till tender. Drain. Puree or process
until fine texture is obtained. Add other
ingredients. Roll into balls covering with bran.
Place on lightly floured or greased tray, flatten
slightly. Bake for 20-25 minutes on 190°C.

	Per Serve
Protein	17 g
Calcium	139 mg
Iron	5.5 mg

Wheat, Dairy and Egg Free

79

HIJIKI PIE

Serves 4

Base:
¾ cup rice flour
¾ cup rolled millet flakes
1 tbs savoury nutritional yeast flakes or 1 vegetable cube
5 – 6 tbs water (if using cube, dissolve in water)

Filling:
½ cup chopped hijiki
2 onions
2 cloves garlic
1 tsp fresh ginger
2 cups diced pumpkin
2 cups mixed vegetables of choice
2 tbs tamari or soy sauce
2 tsp chopped basil

Topping:
½ cup ground almonds
½ cup rice flour
½ cup millet flour
1 dsp each chives or chopped spring onions, basil, herbs
Tamari
1/3 cup water

Base: mix flour and flakes with seasoning and water. Pat into a lightly greased 23 cm pie plate to make the crust.
Lightly steam the vegetables.
Add other filling ingredients and pile into shell.
Mix topping ingredients to a crumble and sprinkle over the pie filling.
Bake at 180°C for approximately 30 minutes.

	Per Serve
Protein	12 g
Calcium	133 mg
Iron	3 mg

Wheat, Dairy and Egg Free

HOMMOUS

1 x 400 g can chick peas drained
1 tsp chopped garlic
1 tbs tamari or soy sauce
2 tbs lemon juice
2 tbs water
1 tbs olive oil

Place all ingredients in a food processor or blend with a Bamix type wand until smooth.

	Per Serve
Protein	45 g
Calcium	300 mg
Iron	12 mg

LENTIL & CARROT LOAF

Serves 4

1 cup lentils (uncooked)
1 cup diced carrots
¼ cup finely chopped spring onions
½ cup chopped almonds
¾ cup rolled oats
½ tsp sage
1 tbs tamari
2 tbs chopped parsley
1 tsp Herbamare (optional)

Cook and drain lentils.
Steam carrots.
Mash carrots and lentils, roughly.
Combine with all remaining ingredients.
Pack firmly into casserole or greased loaf tin lined with oat bran and bake for approximately 30-40 minutes in a moderate 180°C oven.
After removing from oven let the loaf stand for at least 5 minutes before turning out.

	Per Serve
Protein	15 g
Calcium	73 mg
Iron	4.5 mg

Dairy and Egg Free

LENTIL BOLOGNAISE SAUCE

Serves 4

1 cup lentils (uncooked)
1 cup diced onion
2 cloves crushed garlic
3 cups chopped mushrooms
2 cups chopped tomatoes
1 cup tomato puree
1 tbs water
1 tsp dried marjoram
2 bay leaves
2 tsp tamari

Cook and drain lentils.
Saute onions and garlic in a little
water until soft.
Add the mushrooms, cooked lentils, marjoram
and bay leaves and cook for a further 10
minutes.
Stir in tomatoes and tomato puree.
Cover and cook for 20-25 minutes.
Remove bay leaves and puree the remaining
mixture briefly to obtain a sauce-like
consistency.
Season with tamari.
Serve over spaghetti.

	Per Serve
Protein	12 g
Calcium	54 mg
Iron	4 mg

Wheat, Dairy and Egg Free

LENTIL PIE

Serves 4

Base:

1½ cups organic brown rice
½ cup savoury Nutritional yeast flakes
½ cup rice flour

Filling:

400 g sweet potato (gold), diced
2 leeks, chopped
500 mls stock or water
50 g button mushrooms
1½ cups brown, green or red lentils
1 tsp crushed garlic
½ cup chopped, soaked arame seaweed
2 tbs chopped, fresh coriander or 1 tsp dried
1 tsp cumin powder
1 tsp Herbamare or 1 dsp soy sauce

Topping:

1 cup oatmeal
2 tsp mixed herbs
2 tsp yeast flakes

Mix together.

Preheat oven to 200°C.
Cook the rice in plenty of water
until quite soft.
Drain, don't rinse.
Add flakes and rice flour. Line a 20 cm greased
pie dish, base and sides with the rice mixture.
Blind bake for 15 minutes.
Saute the leeks in a little water, add 500 mls
(2½ cups of water or stock).
Add lentils and cook 25 minutes.
Add mushrooms and sweet potato, cook
5 minutes then add seasonings and arame,
stirring occasionally.
Pile mix into rice base and sprinkle on topping.
Bake in oven 30 minutes until hot and
brown on top.

	Per Serve
Protein	18 g
Calcium	85 mg
Iron	4.6 mg

Wheat, Dairy and Egg Free

LENTIL PIE (2)

Serves 4

1 cup diced onion
1 cup diced carrot
1 cup brown lentils
½ cup rice flour
1 cup tomato puree
1 kilo potatoes (cooked and mashed)
1 cup diced pumpkin
1 cup diced parsnip
1 tsp chopped garlic
1 tbs tamari or soy sauce
vegetable salt for taste
1 tbs curry powder

Cook lentils after soaking overnight.
Lightly steam carrot, onion, pumpkin, and parsnip.
Cook drain and mash potatoes in another saucepan.
Mix all ingredients together, except potato.
Grease baking dish with unsalted butter.
Put mixture into baking dish.
Top with mashed potato.
Bake in moderately hot oven until brown (approx 30-40 minutes).

	Per Serve
Protein	15 g
Calcium	82 mg
Iron	6 mg

Wheat, Dairy and Egg Free

LENTIL PIKELETS WITH MUSHROOM SALSA

Serves 4

Pikelets:

1 cup brown lentils
1 cup rice flour
1 tsp baking powder
1 tsp caraway seeds
1 egg (optional)
½ tsp Herbamare
¾ cup soy or oat milk (may need a little more if not using egg)

Cook lentils in boiling water then drain.
Sift flour and baking powder into a bowl and add combined egg and milk, beat well, add Herbamare and lentils.
Heat and grease a heavy pan with unsalted butter and drop 2 tablespoons of mix into pan, cook until bubbles rise then turn over and cook other side.

	Per Serve
Protein	14 g
Calcium	40 mg
Iron	3.5 mg

Mushroom Salsa:

1 medium green capsicum
1 medium red capsicum
1 finely chopped red onion
2 cups sliced mushrooms, can use shiitake
½ tsp Herbamare
1 tbs fresh thyme leaves

Quarter capsicum, remove seeds and membranes and slice.
Saute mushrooms and onion in a little water, add capsicum.
Cook for 2 minutes, add seasoning.
Serve with pikelets.

	Per Serve
Protein	2 g
Calcium	21 mg
Iron	1 mg

**Wheat and Dairy Free
(if using soy or oat milk)
Can be Egg Free**

82

LENTIL ROLLS

Serves 3-4

3 cups cooked brown lentils
3 cups cooked, lightly mashed, mixed vegetables,
eg. (broccoli, carrots, parsnips & potatoes)
1 chopped onion, cooked or ½ cup chopped
spring onions, chopped
1 tbs tamari
Any other seasoning of choice
4 sheets filo pastry or 4 pieces mountain bread
or 4 serves of cooked rice

Mix can be used in moulds with sauce
when serving.
Unmould onto a bed of lettuce and decorate
with slices of tomato etc. (individual plates)
Or mix all ingredients together and roll in filo
sheets folded in half or in mountain bread.
Cut in 5 cm logs.
Bake for 15-20 minutes at 180°C.

Tomato Yoghurt Sauce:
1 cup yoghurt
1 tsp crushed garlic
½ tsp mustard (hot English)
¾ cup sundried tomatoes, chopped

Bamix garlic, mustard and tomatoes.
Mix into yoghurt.

	Per Serve
Protein	92 g
Calcium	586 mg
Iron	48 mg

LENTIL SPREAD

½ cup red or green lentils
½ cup chick peas or lima beans (can use tinned)
2 tsp curry powder
2 tsp coriander powder
2 tsp chopped garlic
2 tbs lemon juice

2 tbs braggs bouillon
½ tsp Herbamare
2 tbs flax oil
Water

Drain chick peas or tinned beans.
Bring to the boil and simmer until peas are soft.
Cover lentils with water and cook until soft.
Rinse beans or chick peas and lentils.
Puree them in a blender, adding the rest of the
ingredients, slowly adding enough water to mix
to cream consistency.

	Per Serve
Protein	18.5 g
Calcium	101 mg
Iron	5 mg

Wheat, Dairy and Egg Free

LIMA BEAN LOAF

2 cups lima beans
½ cup soft breadcrumbs
½ cup chopped parsley
½ tsp chopped garlic
1 tsp Herbamare
½ tsp sage
½ cup tomato juice
2 beaten eggs
1 tbs olive oil (optional)

Soak lima beans overnight in cold water.
Drain and cook in fresh water until soft.
Drain and mash beans roughly and mix with all
other ingredients.
Place in a lightly greased loaf pan in moderate
oven 180°C for 35-40 minutes.
Serve with green vegetables or a salad.

	Per Serve
Protein	18 g
Calcium	67 mg
Iron	3 mg

Dairy Free
Wheat Free (if using rice bread)

83

MACARONI BAKE

Serves 4

200 g rice macaroni or spirals
2 cups diced carrot
2 cups diced zucchini
2 cups diced celery
2 cups milk
¼ cup cornflour
1 cup grated cheese
1 tsp vegetable seasoning
Parsley

Cook pasta. Steam vegetables.
Heat 1½ cups milk in a pan.
Dissolve cornflour in remaining ½ cup milk.
Stir cornflour mix into hot milk, stirring until boiling and boil for 1 minute.
Add vegetable seasoning and steamed vegetables. Mix macaroni and white sauce into vegetables, place in a greased casserole dish, sprinkle cheese on top and bake in oven at 180° C for 30 minutes.
Top with chopped parsley.

	Per Serve
Protein	10 g
Calcium	327 mg
Iron	5 mg
Saturated Fat	6 g

Wheat and Egg Free

MACARONI CHEESE

Serves 4

1 large can tomato soup
200 g grated cheese
1 small onion, chopped
200 g cooked macaroni
½ cup milk of choice
250 g ham or bacon (optional)
1 cup soft breadcrumbs

Heat soup and milk together.
Add half the grated cheese.
Saute onion and ham or bacon
and add to soup.
Add macaroni to soup and pour into baking dish.
Top with bread crumbs and grated cheese and bake in moderate oven 20 minutes.

	Per Serve
Protein	18 g
Calcium	415 mg
Iron	3 mg
Saturated Fat	12 gm

Egg Free

MEXICAN RICE

Serves 4

2 cups brown or white rice
3 cups water or stock
2 small onions, chopped
1 clove of garlic, chopped
1 cup chopped red capsicum
3 medium tomatoes, chopped
1 tbs tomato puree
3 small carrots, sliced
2 tbs fresh coriander, chopped

Cook rice in stock or water.
Sauté onion and garlic in small amount of water, add capsicum and carrots.
Cook covered until carrots are tender, for about 10 minutes.
Cook chopped tomato, tomato puree and coriander for 10 minutes.
Drain rice and add vegetables.
Pour tomato sauce over rice to serve.

	Per Serve
Protein	9 g
Calcium	61 mg
Iron	1.5 mg

Wheat, Dairy and Egg Free

MILLET BURGERS

Serves 4

3 cups cooked millet
1 cup finely grated carrot
1 onion, chopped
1 clove garlic, chopped
¼ cup whole grain breadcrumbs
½ cup ground almonds
1 tbs tamari
¾ tsp thyme or marjoram
1 tsp sage

Lightly saute carrot, garlic and onion in water.
Cover and cook on low heat for 5 minutes.
In a bowl mix with other ingredients.
Shape into burgers. If too crumbly add a little
water till they hold together well.
Bake on a greased oven tray until browned
(approx 20 minutes).

	Per Serve
Protein	26 g
Calcium	118 mg
Iron	14.5 mg

Dairy and Egg Free
Wheat Free (if using rice breadcrumbs)

MUESLI

Serves 2

2 cups rolled oats or mixture of flaked grains
½ cup sultanas
½ cup currants
½ cup almonds, roughly chopped
1 cup biodynamic apple or pear juice

Mix all dry ingredients well.
Store in a covered jar until ready for use.
Pour juice over muesli and allow to soak for a
short while before eating.

	Per Serve
Protein	19 g
Calcium	118 mg
Iron	14 mg

Wheat, Dairy and Egg Free

OAT RISSOLES

Serves 2

2 cups oats – soaked in cold water 15 minutes,
then strained
1 cup spelt flour
1 medium onion, chopped
1 tbs chopped parsley
1 tsp mixed herbs
2 tbs tamari sauce
1 tsp curry powder
1 egg or a little water to bind mix.
Optional - rice flour or breadcrumb coating

Mix all except last ingredient well together
and shape into burgers.
Can be rolled in rice flour or breadcrumbs.
Place on greased oven tray and bake for 20
minutes at 180°C.

	Per Serve
Protein	5 g
Calcium	25 mg
Iron	1 mg

Dairy Free

ORIENTAL PASTA

Serves 4

1 packet rice pasta spirals, cooked
6 mushrooms sliced
¾ cup carrots julienne
½ thinly sliced red capsicum
½ cup parsnip julienne
1 cup diced cabbage
1 onion, cut into wedges
2 tbs lemon juice
1 tbs each honey, grated ginger root and vinegar
1 tbs tamari and 1 tbs water
Dash cayenne
2 cloves garlic, crushed

Steam all vegetables except mushrooms.
Cook mushrooms in tamari-water for about 10 minutes and strain.
Mix mushrooms with steamed vegetables and pasta.
Stir together honey, ginger, cayenne, lemon juice, garlic.
Pour over pasta and vegetables, mix gently.
Can be served hot or cold.

	Per Serve
Protein	5.5 g
Calcium	26 mg
Iron	2 mg

Dairy, Egg and Gluten Free

POLENTA WEDGES

Makes 48 small Triangles

1 litre water
1¾ cups yellow polenta
¾ cup yeast flakes (Lotus brand)
2 tbs chopped sundried tomatoes

Lightly grease 20 cm x 30 cm pan with unsalted butter or olive oil.
Bring water to boil in a saucepan.
When boiling, slowly add the polenta, stirring constantly.
Reduce the heat and simmer, stirring for 15 minutes.
Add the yeast flakes and chopped tomatoes.
Spoon the polenta into the greased pan and smooth the top with the back of a wet spoon.
Mark into 24 x 3 cm squares and allow to set for one hour.
Turn out of pan carefully and cut into the squares and then cut diagonally through each square making a triangle.
The polenta can be used as is or can be toasted under a hot grill for a few minutes on each side.
Alternatively bake in a hot oven for 15 minutes before cutting.
Use as a snack or as part of a main meal with salad or hot vegetables.

	Per Serve
Protein	13 g
Calcium	62 mg
Iron	7.9 mg

Wheat, Dairy and Egg Free

POLENTA

Serves 2-3

½ cup cooked brown rice
1 cup vegetable stock or water
½ cup soy or oat milk
½ cup yellow polenta
¼ cup toasted, chopped almonds
½ tsp Herbamare
2 tsp chopped fresh basil or 1 tsp dried basil

Bring stock and milk to boil in a pan, stir in polenta and simmer about 10 minutes stirring constantly.
Add rice, almonds, basil and Herbamare.
Mix well.
Spread mixture evenly on baking tray.
Mark into triangles.
Cook in a moderate oven 10-15 minutes.

	Per Serve
Protein	16 g
Calcium	87 mg
Iron	4.5 mg

RED LENTIL PATTIES

Serves 4

2 cups cold cooked red lentils
2 cups cold mashed potatoes
½ cup finely diced carrots
½ cup finely diced onions
¼ cup water
½ cup fine dry breadcrumbs or rice bran

Saute carrots and onions in water for 3 minutes. Pour off excess liquid, if any, remove and from heat.
Transfer sauteed vegetables to a mixing bowl and combine with lentils and mashed potato.
Shape into 8 patties and coat with bread crumbs.
Place on greased oven tray.
Bake at 200°C for 20 minutes, turning once, until golden on both sides.
Serve hot or cold with vegetables or salad.

	Per Serve
Protein	20 g
Calcium	55 mg
Iron	1 mg

Dairy & Egg Free
Wheat Free (if using rice bran)

SAVOURY CRUMBLE TOPPING

1 cup rolled oats
1 tbs soy mayonnaise
1 dsp tamari
1 tsp mixed herbs

Coarsely grind the oats and mix in the herbs.
Combine the mayonnaise and tamari, then add to the oat mix. Use as required.

SAVOURY STUFFED BREAD

Serves 4

1 unsliced square loaf of bread.

Stuffing:

3 cups cooked red lentils (drained)
1 cup finely chopped parsley
1 cup diced carrots
½ cup diced red capsicum
1 cup diced onions
3 cloves garlic, finely chopped
1 tbs tomato paste
¼ cup water

Cut crust from one end of loaf.
Scoop out and discard centre.
Keep crust.
To make stuffing, combine all ingredients, except lentils in a large saucepan.
Saute for 5 minutes in the water then cover with lid and cook gently for a further 5 minutes, stirring often to prevent sticking.
Remove from heat and stir in lentils.
Mix thoroughly.
Press stuffing into cavity of loaf, pressing down firmly.
Replace crust and bake on a tray for 40 minutes in 200°C oven.
Set aside for 10 minutes before cutting.
To serve remove crusts from both ends and slice thickly.

	Per Serve
Protein	98 g
Calcium	542 mg
Iron	25 mg

Dairy and Egg Free

SPLIT PEAS & LENTIL BURGERS

Serves 4

1 cup brown lentils
1 cup yellow split peas
1 grated onion
3 tsp fresh thyme
1 cup breadcrumbs
2 tsp mustard
2 tsp horseradish cream

Cover lentils and split peas with water and cook until tender. Drain. Saute the onions.
Puree half the lentils and split peas until combined.
Remove from blender and place in bowl.
Add the remaining peas, lentils, sauteed onion, breadcrumbs, mustard and thyme.
Mix well – if too wet add a little rice flour.
Make burgers and place on greased trays.
Cook for ½ hour in medium oven 180°C.
Serve with mustard sauce

Mustard Sauce:
3 tbs soy mayonnaise
2 tsp horseradish cream
1 tsp prepared mustard (hot English)
Mix together well.

	Per Serve
Protein	20 g
Calcium	50 mg
Iron	4.5 mg

Dairy and Egg Free
Wheat Free (if using rice bread)

88

TACO BEANS

Serves 4

*2 cups Borlotti beans, soaked overnight
in cold water
2 onions
1 red and 1 green capsicum
4 tomatoes
2 cups chopped mushrooms
2 tbs mixed herbs
2 tsp chopped garlic
1 tsp oregano
½ cup water
1 tbs cornflour dissolved in ½ cup cold water*

Pour soak water off beans, cover with fresh
cold water and boil gently till tender, then drain.
Roughly chop all vegetables and simmer in ½
cup of water with lid on pan, for 2 minutes.
Add seasonings.
Cook further 10 minutes.
Add beans to sauce, and reheat.
Thicken with cornflour mix if necessary.

	Per Serve
Protein	10.5 g
Calcium	66 mg
Iron	3 mg

Wheat, Dairy and Egg Free

TOFU RECIPES

SLICED TOFU WITH GINGER

Serves 4

*300 g tofu
Tamari
Water
1 teaspoon grated green ginger
1 medium brown onion*

Cut tofu into slices eg. 10cm × 7cm × 1.5cm thick.
Place in a baking dish with finely grated ginger
and diced brown onions on top.
Add a mixture of 50/50 tamari with water.
Pour on to just cover the tofu and bake for 10
minutes in a hot oven or until browning on top.
Serve with steamed green leafy vegetables and
brown rice.

	Per Serve
Protein	4 g
Calcium	70 mg
Iron	1 mg

TOFU DIP

Serves 8

*2 cups tofu
1 tbs yeast flakes
2 tsp tamari
½ tsp cumin
1 dsp chopped parsley
1 dsp chopped celery
2 tbs cider vinegar
½ tsp turmeric
1 tbs soy yoghurt*
Blend all ingredients together.

	Per serve
Protein	28.4 g
Calcium	446 mg
Iron	5 mg

Wheat, Dairy and Egg Free

89

SPANIKOPITA

Serves 4

1 bunch spinach (washed, cooked and chopped)
1 bunch silverbeet, white stalks removed, (as above)
2 onions, chopped and sauteed
1½ cups tofu, crumbled
1 tsp tamari
1 tsp crushed garlic
½ cup white sauce or 1 egg to bind
½ dsp oregano
2 tbs lemon juice
8 sheets filo pastry

Mix all ingredients except pastry.
Place 2 sheets pastry together and cut in half lengthways. Put about ½ cup of spinach mixture onto filo pastry on lower left corner. Fold filling in, forming a triangle, repeat with rest of filling. Put on a greased oven tray, cook in moderate oven until browned and heated through, about 15 minutes.

	Per Serve
Protein	8.5 g
Calcium	151 mg
Iron	3.5 mg

Dairy and Egg Free

SWEET & SOUR TEMPEH OR TOFU

Serves 4

1 block tempeh or tofu cut into 1½ cm cubes
2 large carrots, thinly sliced
½ cup mirin (sweet & sour sauce)
1 large red and 1 large green capsicum
2 tsp freshly grated green ginger
½ cup tamari
½ cup water

Marinate tofu or tempeh in tamari, ginger and water for 30 minutes, then heat gently.

Steam capsicums and carrots till just tender.
Remove tempeh or tofu from marinade and mix marinade with the mirin. Reheat.
Pour the marinade over the steamed vegetables and tofu or tempeh that has been placed on a bed of rice or noodles.

	Per Serve
Protein	14 g
Calcium	43 mg
Iron	2.5 mg

Wheat, Dairy and Egg Free

TEMPEH STIR FRY

1 block unseasoned tempeh
1 cup each of sliced cabbage, broccoli, carrots, zucchini and sweet potato or pumpkin
1 onion, chopped
2 cloves garlic, crushed
½ cup water
Juice 1 lemon
1 dsp olive oil
1 tbs tamari or soy sauce

Cut tempeh into 1 cm blocks.
Saute in ½ cup tamari and ½ cup water adding onion and garlic.
Simmer for 10 minutes.
Add vegetables (and 2 extra tbs water if needed), and simmer with lid on for 5 – 10 minutes until cooked but still crisp.
Add olive oil and lemon juice and mix.
Serve with a cooked grain or pasta.

	Per Serve
Protein	12 g
Calcium	58 mg
Iron	1.5 mg

Wheat, Dairy and Egg Free

TOFU OR TEMPEH AND AVOCADO SPREAD OR DIP

1 avocado
100 g seasoned tempeh or tofu

If using tempeh, crumble and sauté in a pan with a little water (2 tbs) for 10 minutes.
Tofu can be used as is.
Peel and roughly chop avocado.
Place both ingredients in a food processor and process until smooth.

	Per Serve
Protein	7 g
Calcium	100 mg
Iron	6 mg

TOFU RICE BURGERS

Serves 4

1 block tofu (approximately 300 g)
½ cup chopped parsley
1 tbs mixed herbs
½ cup chopped spring onions
1 cup grated carrot
1 dsp miso
3 cups cooked rice
(puree ½ rice after cooking)
1 tsp crushed garlic

Mash tofu.
Mix all ingredients together.
Make into 8 burgers.
Place on greased tray and brown in oven, for about 20 minutes at 200°C turning once.

	Per Serve
Protein	12 g
Calcium	140 mg
Iron	1.75 mg

Wheat, Dairy and Egg Free

TOFU TOMATO SPREAD

Serves 4

1 cup tofu
¼ cup chopped tomato
½ tsp dried basil
½ tsp dried marjoram
¼ tsp herbamare

Place all ingredients in food processor and blend until smooth.
If using fresh herbs, double quantity to 1 teaspoon.

	Per Serve
Protein	8.5 g
Calcium	135 mg
Iron	1.5 mg

Wheat, Dairy and Egg Free

91

TOFU TRIANGLES

Makes 8

4 sheets filo pastry

Filling:

200 g organic tofu (firm)
½ cup chopped spring onions
¼ cup chopped coriander leaves
¼ cup grated fresh green ginger
1 dsp tamari
1 clove garlic, crushed
1 cup grated carrot
½ cup green peas
¼ cup rice flour
½ cup soaked arame, chopped
1 egg, lightly beaten (optional)

Preheat oven to 180°C.
Mix all ingredients together, except egg.
Lay two sheets filo together, cut into 4 oblongs.
Repeat with the other 2 sheets or line a pie plate with the two sheets.
Divide mixture into 8 and place one portion on each oblong, roll up into triangles and place on a greased tray. Brush with egg.
Or pile all mixture into lined pie plate and top with 2 sheets filo, (brushing base edge with egg before adding top sheets).
Pinch edges together and brush top with egg.
Prick top with fork or cut several slits.
Bake approximately 30 minutes.

	Per Serve
Protein	7 g
Calcium	66 mg
Iron	2 mg

Dairy Free

VEGETABLE TOFU OR TEMPEH BURGERS

Serves 4

½ cup grated pumpkin
½ cup grated carrot
½ cup grated parsnip
½ cup cooked rice
1 cup tofu or tempeh, crumbled (tempeh must be marinated and cooked first)
1 tsp lemon rind
1 tsp lemon juice
1 tbs tamari
1 cup wholemeal breadcrumbs
1 tsp crushed garlic
1 tsp coriander
1 tsp barley miso dissolved in water

Steam vegetables lightly. Mash tofu and the rest of the ingredients and mix well.
Form into patties and place on a greased oven tray and bake in the oven for 30 minutes turning once.
This mix can be placed in a greased loaf pan and baked in a moderate oven until browned.
In this recipe any cooked grain or legume can be used in place of tofu or tempeh.

	Per Serve
Protein	5.3 g
Calcium	40 mg
Iron	0.75 mg

Dairy and Egg Free

BEEF & LAMB RECIPES

BEEF AND BEAN CASSEROLE

Serves 4

750 g blade steak
315 g can red kidney beans or 1½-2 cups home cooked kidney beans
2 tbs plain flour of choice
½ tsp sea salt or Herbamare vegetable salt
2 tbs olive oil and 2 tbs water, mixed
2 cups chopped tomatoes
1 cup red capsicum strips
2 cloves garlic, crushed
2 onions, sliced
1 tbs Worcestershire sauce
2 tbs apple cider vinegar
1 tbs honey
½ cup water

Cube steak after removing excess fat.
Coat in flour and seasoning.
Heat oil and water in a pan and
brown the meat.
Place in a casserole dish.
Mix the tomatoes, garlic, Worcestershire sauce,
vinegar, honey, water and onion.
Pour over the meat, cover and cook in a
moderate oven for approximately 1 hour.
Add kidney beans and capsicum, return to
oven and cook a further ¾ hour.
Serve with potatoes and green vegetables.

	Per Serve
Protein	48 g
Calcium	89 mg
Iron	13 mcg
Saturated Fat	5 g

Wheat, Dairy and Egg Free

BEEF CASSEROLE

Serves 4

500 g fat free beef, cut into 2 cm cubes
1 tbs oil and 1 tbs water
1 large onion, chopped
2 stalks celery, sliced
2 carrots and 2 parsnips, sliced diagonally
1 cup peas
1 tsp crushed garlic
2 bay leaves
300 mls water
2 stock cubes (or 1 tsp vegetable stock powder)
2 tsp cornflour and a little extra water

Saute cubed beef in 1 tbs oil and 1 tbs water.
Add onion, cook with lid on for 15 minutes,
stirring occasionally.
Add water and stock cubes and all other
ingredients.
Replace lid and simmer 45 minutes.
Thicken sauce with 2 tsp cornflour dissolved in
a little water.
Boil for 2 minutes. Remove bay leaves.
Serve with mashed potato, broccoli or brown
rice.

	Per Serve
Protein	26 g
Calcium	79 mg
Iron	5 mg
Saturated Fat	5 g

Wheat, Dairy and Egg Free

BEEF CHOW MEIN

Serves 4

500 g round steak
1 tbs corn flour mixed in 2 tbs dry sherry
or water
1 stalk celery, sliced
½ cup each sliced red and green capsicum
125 g sliced green beans
125 g sliced mushrooms
1 tbs tamari or soy sauce
1 tbs oil and 1 tbs water

Slice steak very thinly.
Marinate for 10 minutes in corn flour mixture.
Heat oil and water in a pan.
Add beef strips and cook for 5 minutes, browning well.
Remove from pan, add a little more water if necessary to the pan and cook vegetables for 5 minutes.
Add tamari and beef strips and heat through.
Serve with boiled rice or noodles.

	Per Serve
Protein	24 gr
Calcium	36 mg
Iron	5 mg
Saturated fat	8.4 mg

Wheat, Dairy & Egg Free

BEEF OR LAMB PILAF

Serves 4

500 g thinly sliced lamb (or beef)
1 large brown onion sliced
2 cups diced carrots
2 cups diced zucchini
1 cup sliced celery
1 tsp cumin
1 tsp coriander
1 tsp sweet paprika
½ tsp salt
2 cups basmati rice
2 vegetable stock cubes
2 cups water

Saute onion and spices in 2 tbs olive oil and 2 tbs water in a large pan.
Add the washed rice and stir constantly until the rice is golden and coated in the oil.
Add the 2 cups of water and crushed vegetable stock cube, carrot, zucchini and celery.
Stir occasionally and cook until vegetables are tender about 10-15 minutes.
Saute or grill lamb or beef strips for 10 minutes.
Stir meat into the cooked vegetables and rice and serve topped with chopped parsley.

	Per Serve
Protein	17 g
Calcium	64 mg
Iron	4 mg
Saturated fat	8.4 g

Wheat, Dairy and Egg Free

CITRUS LAMB CHOPS

Serves 4

4 – 6 lamb chump chops
1 tbs vinegar
½ tsp ground ginger
½ tsp sea salt
1 tsp each grated lemon rind and grated orange rind
1 tbs cornflour
1 tbs butter or oil and 1 tbs water
1 tbs honey or brown sugar
¾ cup orange juice

Heat butter or oil with water in a pan.
Brown chops on both sides.
Add combined vinegar, sugar, ginger and salt.
Cover and simmer for 30 minutes.
Remove chops and keep warm.
Blend cornflour with orange juice and rinds.
Heat, stirring until the sauce boils and thickens.
Pour over chops and serve with rice or pasta and cooked greens.

	Per Serve
Protein	22 g
Calcium	28 mg
Iron	1 mg
Saturated Fat	5 g

Wheat, Dairy and Egg Free

LAMB & PUMPKIN CASSEROLE

Serves 4

6 lamb forequarter chops
1 large red onion cut into wedges
1 tsp crushed garlic
½ cup apple cider vinegar
½ tsp cinnamon
900 g butternut pumpkin cut into 3 cm cubes
2 tbs honey
½ tsp salt or 1 tsp Herbamare

Saute onion in 1 tbs olive oil and 1 tbs water over gentle heat in a casserole dish.
Add vinegar and cinnamon.
Seal chops on both sides in the onion vinegar mix.
Cover casserole dish with a tightly fitting lid and place in a preheated oven 180°C for 30 minutes.
Uncover and scatter diced pumpkin over meat and drizzle with honey.
Cook for a further 45 minutes and serve with a green leafy vegetable and rice.

	Per Serve
Protein	20 g
Calcium	57 mg
Iron	2 mg
Saturated Fat	8 g

Wheat, Dairy and Egg Free

MEAT AND VEGETABLE PASTA SAUCE

Serves 4

250 g fat free minced steak
1 large onion, chopped
2 stalks celery, thinly sliced
2 carrots, grated
4 tomatoes or 1 small tin tomatoes
1 bay leaf
2 tsp dried basil
1 tsp crushed garlic

Saute chopped onion in a little water (¼ cup) until light brown.
Add meat and break up with a wooden spoon, saute until colour change.
Add chopped tomatoes and other ingredients. Stir to combine well and simmer with the lid on for 20 – 30 minutes, stirring occasionally.
Serve over pasta of choice.
Top with a sprinkle of parsley and/or Parmesan cheese.

	Per Serve
Protein	5 g
Calcium	31 mg
Iron	2.5 mcg
Saturated Fat	8 g

Wheat, Dairy and Egg Free

MEAT LOAF

Serves 4

750 g minced beef
250 g sausage mince
4 rashers bacon
1½ cups soft breadcrumbs
1 egg
½ cup chopped spring onion
½ tsp sea salt or 1 dsp tamari sauce
Optional dried breadcrumbs

Combine all ingredients and shape into a log loaf.
Roll in dried breadcrumbs if liked.
Place in a greased pan and cover.
Cook at 175°C for 1 to 1¼ hours.
If liked, pumpkin, potato, carrots and parsnip can be added to the pan after 20 minutes or so.
Turn vegetables and loaf once during cooking.
Serve with a green vegetable or cook alone and serve cold with salad.

	Per Serve
Protein	22 g
Calcium	53 mg
Iron	11.5 mg
Saturated Fat	50 g

Dairy Free

MEAT PLUS RISSOLES

Serves 4

300 g fat free mince steak
I cup each grated carrot and potato
I cup chopped celery
I cup oatmeal
I chopped onion
2 cloves garlic, crushed
I egg
I dsp tamari or soy sauce
2 tbs tomato sauce
I tsp mixed herbs
I tsp Herbamare
Rice flour for coating

Mix all ingredients together (except flour) and divide into 8 portions.
Shape into rissoles and coat in rice flour.
Gently pan fry in lightly oiled pan with lid on, turning once.
Cook approximately 15 minutes on each side.
Mixture can also be packed into an oiled, floured loaf or casserole dish and baked in a moderate oven for 50-60 minutes.
Turn out and slice.
Serve with brown gravy.

	Per Serve
Protein	14 g
Calcium	87 mg
Iron	8 mg
Saturated Fat	24 g

ORIENTAL BEEF

Serves 4

500 g good quality steak (fillet or rump)
4 sticks celery
I egg and I tbs cornflour
2 medium carrots, cut into thin strips
2 medium onions, cut into thin strips
2 tbs arrowroot (wheat free)
2 cups water and 2 stock cubes
¼ cup oil and ¼ cup water
I tbs soy sauce
¼ tsp sea salt

Cut meat into very thin strips.
Beat egg and cornflour together.
Add ¼ tsp sea salt.
Coat meat with egg mixture.
Heat oil and water and fry meat about 10 minutes until golden.
Drain and pour off excess oil/water.
Put meat to one side.
Add vegetables to pan and saute for 3 minutes, then add stock and bring to the boil.
Add soy sauce to arrowroot, stir into the pan and cook until sauce boils and thickens.
Add meat and reheat gently.
Serve over rice or rice noodles.

	Per Serve
Protein	24 g
Calcium	122 mg
Iron	4 mg
Saturated Fat	5 g

Wheat Free

RED LAMB & SPINACH

Serves 4

4 lamb chump chops (trim off fat)
600 g (4 cups) large diced potatoes
800 g can diced tomatoes
1 bunch spinach
3 cups rice of choice
1 tsp crushed garlic
¾ cup pine nuts
1 tsp diced basil or 1 tbs chopped fresh basil

Seal and brown the chops in a large pan for 10 minutes using 1 tbs oil.
Add the tomatoes, potatoes, garlic and simmer with lid on pan for 30 minutes.
Add the pine nuts and basil.
Wash, chop roughly and steam spinach.
Cook rice according to packet instructions.

	Per Serve
Protein	25 g
Calcium	130 mg
Iron	2.5 mg
Saturated Fat	8 g

Wheat, Dairy and Egg Free

SHEPHERD'S PIE

Serves 4

1 kg very lean minced beef
1 large onion, chopped
1 tbs oil and 1 tbs water
2 tbs plain flour of choice
2 beef cubes dissolved in 1½ cups water
1 bouquet garni
½ tsp sea salt
2 tbs tomato paste

Topping:

8 good sized potatoes
Sea salt
Milk
½ cup spring onions, chopped
Parsley chopped

Saute the chopped onion in the heated oil and water. Add the beef, stir and let change colour. Sprinkle in the flour, add the stock and stir gently. Simmer for 30 – 40 minutes.
Add bouquet garni, salt and tomato paste.
Meanwhile, boil the potatoes, drain and mash with a little salt and milk.
Add chopped spring onions.
Remove bouquet garni from meat, place ½ mashed potato in a casserole dish, top with meat mix. Cover with remaining potato, place in moderate oven and cook for ¾ hour.
Remove from oven and sprinkle with chopped parsley. Serve with salad or vegetables of choice.

	Per Serve
Protein	70 g
Calcium	111 mg
Iron	3 mg
Saturated Fat	16 g

**Egg Free and Wheat Free
if using Rice Flour.**

SIMPLE BEEF ON PASTA

Serves 4

1 diced onion
1 tsp crushed garlic
1 cup tomato pasta sauce
½ cup water
2 diced carrots
2 tsp mixed dried herbs
400 g low fat minced beef
4 cups cooked rice or spelt pasta
1 cup freshly grated Parmesan cheese

Saute onion and garlic in a little water or oil.
Add meat and stir until browned.
Add water, pasta sauce, carrots and seasoning.
Simmer for 30 minutes.
Place hot pasta in a bowl, top with meat mix
and garnish with Parmesan.

	Per Serve
Protein	7 g
Calcium	73 mg
Iron	2.8 mg
Saturated Fat	9.5 mg

Wheat and Egg Free

STUFFED VEAL

Serves 4

8 thin veal fillets
Seasoned flour

Stuffing:

125 g mushrooms, finely sliced and sauteed
in a little butter or water
2 tbs chopped onion
½ tsp thyme
½ cup finely chopped celery
¼ tsp sea salt
½ cup ground rice or flour

Sauce:

1 cup chicken or beef stock (2 cubes)
1 dsp tomato paste or puree
1 ½ tbs plain flour of choice
1 dsp Worcestershire or soy sauce
1 clove garlic, crushed

Combine stuffing ingredients.
Pound veal fillets very thin.
Divide stuffing evenly between fillets
and roll up. Secure with a toothpick.
Brown gently on all sides in a little hot butter.
Add the flour to the pan after removing
the veal. Cook 1 minute.
Add rest of ingredients and stir until boiling.

Place veal in a casserole dish and cover with
sauce. Bake at 180°C for approximately
1 hour.

	Per Serve
Protein	32 g
Calcium	14 mg
Iron	1 mg
Saturated Fat	1 g

Wheat, Dairy and Egg Free

99

CHICKEN RECIPES

CHICKEN FRICASSEE

Serves 4

2 large chicken breasts, skinned
1 chopped onion
2 leeks, washed well and sliced
1 cup green peas
1 cup corn kernels
1 cup diced carrot
1 tsp crushed garlic
2 tbs chopped parsley
2 bay leaves
1 chicken or vegetable cube -
dissolved in 2
cups of water
1 large can chicken soup

Slice the chicken breasts in 4 pieces each.
Sauté the pieces in a pan in a little oil until
sealed all over.
Remove the chicken and sauté the
onion and leeks.
Add the rest of the ingredients and cover
stirring occasionally.
Cook for 30 minutes.
Serve over rice.

	Per Serve
Protein	22 g
Calcium	48 mg
Iron	3 mg

Dairy and Egg Free

CHICKEN FRITTERS

Serves 4

2 cups cubed chicken cooked
2 cups buckwheat flour or flour of choice
3 eggs
½ cup chopped spring onion
½ cup milk (approx. may need more)
1 tbs chopped parsley
1 tsp vegetable seasoning
1 cup cooked rice

Place flour in a bowl, make a well in the centre
and pour in the roughly beaten egg and milk.
Gradually incorporate the flour from around
the edges.
Beat well with a spoon to make a smooth
batter, adding a little extra milk if needed.
Stir in the rest of the ingredients.
Heat a small amount of olive oil in a pan and
when hot, drop spoonful in the pan.
Cook until bubbles rise, turn over and cook
the other side.
Serve with vegetables and some sauce.

	Per Serve
Protein	15 g
Calcium	46 mg
Iron	3 mg

Wheat and Dairy Free

CHICKEN LOAF

Serves 4

500 g minced chicken
1 cup green peas
½ cup finely chopped red onion
1 small can mushroom soup
1 cup sliced mushrooms
1 cup grated carrot
1 cup rice
1 tsp chopped garlic

Mix all ingredients together and pack into a greased loaf pan or casserole dish.
Bake at 180°C for 45 – 60 minutes.

	Per Serve
Protein	10 g
Calcium	42 mg
Iron	10 mg
Saturated Fat	4 g

Dairy and Egg Free

CHICKEN RAMEKINS

Serves 4

1 can chicken soup
3 cups cooked, diced chicken
¾ cup chopped walnuts or almonds
1½ cups chopped celery
3 tbs mayonnaise (soy is good)
2 tbs chopped spring onion
2 tbs lemon juice
1 cup grated cheese
1 cup crushed potato chips or breadcrumbs

In a pan, gently heat all ingredients, except the cheese and crumbs, for 10 minutes.
Divide mix between 4 heatproof bowls.
Spread cheese and crumbs over the top and heat in the oven for 30 minutes at 200°C.

	Per Serve
Protein	16.5 g
Calcium	79 mg
Iron	6.5 mg
Saturated Fat	6 g

Egg Free
Wheat Free (if using spelt or rice flour bread)

CHICKEN STIR FRY

Serves 4

400 g chicken breast (skinless)
500 g snow peas, roughly sliced
500 g green beans, chopped into 4 cm lengths
1 red capsicum, cut in thin strips
1 red onion, thinly sliced
2 cups rice
1 tbs olive oil
1 tbs water
Optional extras – tamari or soy sauce, sesame seeds, parsley, nuts

Slice chicken across the grain into strips.
Heat a frypan. Add water and oil.
Saute chicken strips for 5 minutes, then add vegetables. Cover and cook for 10 minutes.
Cook rice in boiling water until soft.
Drain.
Serve chicken and vegetables on the rice, sprinkle with tamari or soy sauce.
Scatter over sesame seeds, parsley or nuts of your choice.

	Per Serve
Protein	22 g
Calcium	77 mg
Iron	2 mg
Saturated Fat	2 g

Wheat, Dairy and Egg Free

101

FISH RECIPES

FISH BAKE
Serves 4

450 g potatoes
1 x 415 g can of tuna or salmon
1½ cups grated cheese
1 x 500 g tin celery or mushroom soup
½ cup chopped parsley
2 cups fresh breadcrumbs, season with
cheese and herbs of choice

Cook potatoes and mash - no butter or milk.
Mix with fish and place in casserole dish.
Add chopped parsley and heat the undiluted
soup. Pour over the soup mix, cover with
breadcrumbs, bake in hot oven for 15 minutes.

	Per serve
Protein	10 g
Calcium	41 mg
Iron	4 mg

Egg Free

FISH PIE

Serves 4

2 – 3 cups cooked flaked fish
1 cup chopped spring onion
1 egg
6 cups mashed potato
½ cup tomato sauce
1 tsp mustard

Mix 1 cup of the potato with the rest of
the ingredients. Place in a casserole dish or
individual ovenproof bowls.
Top with the rest of the potato and heat
through in a moderate oven 180°C until top is
browned. Lunch or entrée dish.

	Per Serve
Protein	4 g
Calcium	94 mg
Iron	1.5 mg

Wheat, Dairy and Egg Free

FISH ROLLS

1 small can tuna or salmon
1 cup cooked rice
2 cups cooked sweet potato
1 cup cooked parsnip
½ cup spring onion
2 sheets low fat flaky pastry

Mash potatoes and parsnip, drain fish.
Mix fish, rice and vegetables together.
Roll pastry a little thinner and cut
each square into 4.
Divide mixture evenly between the 8 squares.
Roll up pastry tucking in the ends as you go,
diagonally works well.
Prick with a fork, put on greased tray and cook
for 30 minutes at 200°C.

	Per Serve
Protein	10 g
Calcium	41 mg
Iron	4 mg

Dairy and Egg Free

GRILLED WHITING

Serves 4

8 small fillets of whiting or fish of choice
Seasoned flour (Herbamare is good)
1 lemon cut in wedges

Coat fillets in seasoned flour.
Place under the grill on a greased solid tray.
Cook until golden, turn and cook other side.
Serve with salad and lemon wedges.

	Per Serve
Protein	20 g

FISHY PASTA

Serves 4

440 g can tuna in spring water,
drained and flaked
1 cup green peas
1 cup corn kernels
1 cup plain yoghurt
1 cup tomato pasta sauce
½ cup chopped spring onions
1 cup breadcrumbs
1 cup grated cheese
1 packet pasta of choice – rice pasta goes well
with this dish

Combine first 6 ingredients and place in a
greased casserole dish.
Mix crumbs and cheese and sprinkle on top of
tuna mix. Bake in oven at 180°C for
30 minutes.
Serve with cooked pasta alongside on plate.

	Per Serve
Protein	36 g
Calcium	200 mg
Iron	2 mg
Saturated Fat	4 g

Wheat and Egg Free
(if using rice pasta)

SALMON OR TUNA PATE

1 cup canned beans (Lima or Cannelloni)
2 tbs chopped parsley
2 tbs lemon juice
1 cup salmon or tuna canned

Blend all together and serve on toast.

Protein	74 g
Calcium	132 mg
Iron	8 mg

GINGERED FISH

Serves 4

750 g Nile perch fillets
2 carrots
2 bunches baby bok choy
1 tsp crushed garlic
5 cm piece of green ginger
2 tsp fish sauce
1 tsp sugar
1½ cups jasmine rice

Cut the fish fillets in half crossways.
Thinly slice the carrots lengthways.
Trim the stalks off the bok choy and wash.
Grate the green ginger.
Cook the rice according to packet directions
Preheat oven to 180°C.
Mix the fish sauce, garlic, ginger and sugar
in a bowl.
Grease baking pan and place ¼ sliced carrot
in one corner.
Pile on ¼ bok choy.
Place 2 pieces of fish on the top and drizzle
¼ of the sauce over.
Repeat in each corner.
Cover and cook for approximately
25-30 minutes.
Uncover and place each fish stack on the bed
of rice on each plate.
Pour any pan juices over the stacks.

	Per Serve
Protein	41 g
Calcium	264 mg
Iron	4 mg

Wheat, Dairy and Egg Free

MOCK SALMON SUSHI

2 toasted sushi nori sheets
1 third of a cup of minced celery
1 cup grated carrot
¼ cup spring onions - chopped
1 cup almonds, soaked in water overnight,
drained, then ground finely
1 tbs liquid aminos, tamari or bouillon
1 tsp kelp powder
3 tbs lemon juice

Finely grate the carrots in a food processor.
Place chop blade in the processor, then put the
grated carrot and the remaining ingredients in
and pulse-chop.
Scrape down the sides of the bowl, then
continue to pulse-chop for a couple of minutes.
Divide the mixture into 2.
Place one half of the mixture along the top of
a toasted nori sheet, roll it up.
Repeat with second half.
Cut each roll into six pieces.
Refrigerate for 1 hour.

SALMON PATTIES

Makes 4 large patties

415 g can pink salmon (flaked)
½ cup chopped spring onion
½ cup dried breadcrumbs
3 tsp curry powder
2 eggs
½ tsp Herbamare
Flour for coating

Place flaked salmon, onions, breadcrumbs,
curry powder and Herbamare in a bowl.
Mix, add eggs and divide into 4 patties.
Coat in flour and pan fry on a lightly greased
frypan or skillet for 10 minutes on each side.

	Per Serve
Protein	22 g
Calcium	272 mg
Iron	1.75 mcg
Saturated Fat	1.8 g

SALADS

SALAD SALSA

Serves 4

1 medium red onion
2 tsp lemon juice
3 medium tomatoes
1 red capsicum
2 tbs flax seed oil
¼ cup chopped fresh coriander leaves
½ tsp garlic

Finely chop red onion, tomato and capsicum. Add other ingredients. Mix well and refrigerate. Serve in ½ avocado cup.

	Per Serve
Protein	4.5 g
Calcium	61 mg
Iron	4 mg

———•———

BEAN SPROUT SALAD

Serves 4-6

4 cups mung bean sprouts (blanched)
1 cup shredded carrots
1 cup shredded cabbage
½ cup chopped soaked hijiki
3 cups sliced mushrooms
1 cup sliced celery
1 cup sliced spring onions
1 cup almonds
1½ cup ginger almond sauce

Combine all prepared vegetables and stir sauce through.

Ginger Almond Sauce:

3 tbs almond butter
4 tbs lemon juice

1 tbs tamari
2 tbs grated fresh ginger
1 tbs flax oil
2 tsp honey

Blend ingredients until smooth and creamy.

	Per Serve
Protein	13 g
Calcium	171 mg
Iron	3 mg

———•———

COLESLAW

Serves 4

2 cups sliced green cabbage
2 cups sliced red cabbage
1 cup grated carrot
1 cup sweet corn kernels
1 cup diced red capsicum

Dressing: Avocado with lime or lemon

½ avocado, mashed
2 tbs cider vinegar
¼ cup lime juice
2 tsp pressed garlic
3 tbs soy mayonnaise
½ cup water
1 tsp soy sauce

Blend all dressing ingredients together in a food processor or with a Bamix wand. Toss through coleslaw vegetables.

	Per Serve
Protein	5 g
Calcium	40 mg
Iron	4 mg

———•———

CORN SALAD

Serves 4

1½ cups corn kernels
1½ cups chick peas, cooked
1 cup grated carrot
½ cup sliced spring onions
¼ cup chopped fresh mint
Juice of 1 lemon
2 tsp apple cider vinegar

Toss all together and chill.

	Per Serve
Protein	15 g
Calcium	84 mg
Iron	3 mg
Saturated Fat	4 g

Wheat, Dairy and Egg Free

CURRIED VEGETABLE SALAD

200 g snow peas
200 g cauliflower
200 g small carrots
1 small Lebanese cucumber
1 cup mung bean sprouts
1 onion chopped
2/3 cup cream
2/3 cup plain yoghurt
Little butter
Little curry powder

Gently steam cauliflower, carrots, snow peas.
Chop the cucumber and rinse the sprouts.
Saute the onion in the butter for 5 minutes.
Add the curry powder and cook
2-3 more minutes.
Add the cream and heat gently stirring.
Remove from heat and add yoghurt.
Pour the sauce over the cooked vegetables.

	Per Serve
Protein	21 g
Calcium	282 mg
Iron	11.75 mg

Wheat and Egg Free

SEA VEGETABLE SALAD

1 cup sliced dried wakame
1 cup arame, roughly chopped
4-6 shiitake mushrooms (dried)
2 cups chopped cucumber
1 cup sliced yellow or green capsicum
1 large tomato diced

Dressing:

2 tbs vinegar
½ tsp crushed garlic
2 tsp tamari or soy sauce
1 tbs flax oil

Soak sea vegetables and mushrooms in warm water for 15-20 minutes.
Strain off soak water, slice mushrooms.
Mix all ingredients together and chill.

	Per Serve
Protein	5 g
Calcium	270 mg
Iron	2 mg

Wheat, Dairy and Egg Free

SPINACH & PUMPKIN SALAD

Serves 4

2 cups large diced pumpkin, peeled
2 cups Jerusalem artichokes or potatoes, peel
and dice large
150 g small fresh spinach leaves
2 cups sweet corn kernels
1 cup cooked green peas (fresh is best)
1 lettuce heart
½ bunch parsley
6 tbs olive or flax oil
3 tbs apple cider vinegar

Boil the potato and pumpkin until tender.
Wash the spinach and lettuce well.
Drain and cool the cooked vegetables.
Chop the parsley roughly.
Mix the oil and vinegar together.
Mix all vegetables together except greens.
Arrange the greens on the plates, pile the
other vegetables together on the greens.
Pour over dressing.

	Per Serve
Protein	10 g
Calcium	57 mg
Iron	10 mg

Wheat, Dairy and Egg Free

SWEET POTATO SALAD

Serves 4

3 cups sweet potato
½ cup chopped arame
¾ cup soy mayonnaise

Scrub sweet potato and dice large.
Steam until just soft.
Soak arame in warm water for 30 minutes.
Mix the potato and arame together with the
soy mayonnaise. Serve while still warm.

	Per Serve
Protein	4 g
Calcium	103 mg
Iron	2.5 mg

Wheat, Dairy and Egg Free

WARM POTATO SALAD

Serves 4

1 kg small red skinned potatoes (Pontiac)
2 cups halved green beans
1 punnet cherry tomatoes
4 spring onions

Cut potatoes into large dices.
Cut beans into approximately 4 cm lengths.
Halve cherry tomatoes.
Clean and slice spring onions.
Steam potatoes and beans.
Add tomatoes and onions.
Place in a bowl and stir dressing through or
pour over when served.

Dressing:

¾ cup packed basil leaves
½ cup fresh grated Parmesan cheese
½ cup plain yoghurt
½ cup nuts of choice
¼ cup olive or flax seed oil

In a food processor, pulse-chop the nuts, basil
and cheese. Gradually add the oil and remove
from processor and stir in the yoghurt.

	Per Serve
Protein	4 g
Calcium	40 mg
Iron	2 mg

RED CABBAGE SALAD

Serves 4

¼ head of red cabbage, grated
I beetroot, grated
I cup small green peas
Dressing of lemon juice, honey and garlic

Toss all together and chill.

	Per Serve
Protein	4 g
Calcium	32 mg
Iron	3 mg

WARM TUNA SALAD

Serves 4

I pkt (250 g) rice pasta spirals
I 425 g can tuna (or salmon)
I 400 g can chick peas
I red onion sliced thinly
3 tomatoes or 12 cherry tomatoes
2 tbs French dressing
2 tbs chopped parsley

Cook pasta according to packet directions.
Drain tuna and chick peas.
Slice tomatoes or cut cherry tomatoes in half.
Mix all ingredients together gently.

	Per Serve
Protein	50 g
Calcium	160 mg
Iron	8 mg

Wheat, Dairy and Egg Free

SOUPS

AVOCADO GAZPACHO

Serves 6

3 avocados, peeled and chopped
I small red Spanish onion, roughly chopped
I small green capsicum, roughly chopped
I small yellow capsicum , roughly chopped
2 large tomatoes – scrape out seeds and flesh
and put aside
I cup soy yoghurt
2 cups water
2 tbs lemon juice
I tbs apple cider vinegar
¼ tsp sambal oelek
2 cloves garlic, crushed
2 tbs chopped fresh basil
I tbs chopped fresh coriander
Optional – chopped parsley to serve

Blend or process avocados, lemon juice, garlic,
yoghurt, vinegar and sambal oelek until smooth.
Stir in basil and coriander.
Cover and refrigerate for 1 hour.
Blend onion, capsicums, tomato pulp and seeds
with water.
Stir in finely chopped tomato shells.
Combine the two mixtures, stir well and chill.
Garnish with chopped parsley to serve.

	Per Serve
Protein	2.5 g
Calcium	4.8 mg
Iron	2 mg

Wheat, Dairy and Egg Free

BEAN SOUP

Serves 4

10 cm stick wakame
½ cup dried Lima beans (soaked overnight)
½ onion, chopped
1 cup chopped carrots
5 cups water
1 dsp miso dissolved in ½ cup warm water

Drain lima beans and discard soak water.
Cook lima beans and wakame in the 5 cups of
fresh water, add carrots and onions and cook
until tender.
Can be pureed.
Add dissolved miso.

	Per Serve
Protein	6 g
Calcium	57 mg
Iron	1 mg

Wheat, Dairy and Egg Free

BROCCOLI & ALMOND SOUP

Serves 4

4 cups roughly chopped broccoli
1 chopped onion
2 tbs chopped almonds
2 cups water
½ cup soy milk
1 tsp mineral bouillon or 1 vegetable stock cube

Chop onion, put into pan with water.
Bring water to the boil and add broccoli
including chopped stalk. Cook until soft.
Add bouillon and soy milk. Puree. Just before
serving add almonds.

	Per Serve
Protein	8 g
Calcium	106 mg
Iron	2 mg

Wheat, Dairy and Egg Free

CAULIFLOWER SOUP
Serves 4

6 cups roughly chopped cauliflower
3 diced onion
1 tsp cumin powder
1 cup soy milk or milk of choice

Cook onion and cauliflower in enough water
to cover well, cook until soft.
Blend in cumin and soy milk.
Reheat but do not boil.
Serve with chopped parsley.

	Per Serve
Protein	4.5 g
Calcium	51 mg
Iron	1.5 mg

Wheat, Dairy and Egg Free

109

CELERY SOUP

Serves 4

1 chopped onion
½-1 bunch of celery (approx. 8 cups chopped)
1 litre of soy milk
2 tbs Braggs bouillon or 2 beef or vegetable stock cubes
ground fennel seeds
ground celery seeds
pinch mixed spice
Herbamare to taste

Chop onion, sauté in a small amount of water.
Cook until onion is soft. Then add celery.
Add minimal water (2 cups) and simmer until celery is tender.
Add the Braggs mineral bouillon and ½ teaspoon of Herbamare and herbs and spices.
Puree. Add soy milk and re-heat.
Do not boil after adding the soy milk or soup may curdle.

	Per Serve
Protein	11.5 g
Calcium	161 mg
Iron	9 mg

Wheat, Dairy and Egg Free

CURRIED ZUCCHINI SOUP

Serves 4

2 large zucchini (approximately 8-10 cups chopped)
2 onions
1 tbs bouillon
½ tbs curry powder
1 cup soy milk

Chop onions and zucchini, cover with water and cook, with curry powder, until soft, then puree. Add soy milk and bouillon to taste.
Garnish with finely chopped red capsicum.

	Per Serve
Protein	4 g
Calcium	25 mg
Iron	2 mg

Wheat, Dairy and Egg Free

HEARTY WINTER SOUP

Serves 6

1 cup pearl barley
2 onions
4 potatoes
4 carrots
1 parsnip
1 turnip, optional
1 swede, optional
4 stalks celery
8 cups water
1 tsp each basil, marjoram and oregano
1 tsp crushed garlic
2 tbs Braggs bouillon
¼ cup chopped parsley
2 bay leaves

Chop vegetables.
Cook barley and onions with bay leaves in water for about 1 hour.
Add remaining ingredients except bouillon and parsley and cook for a further hour for best results. Add bouillon.
Serve topped with parsley accompanied by crusty bread or toast.
Note: This recipe can be considered a complete nutrient meal.

	Per Serve
Protein	9 gr
Calcium	100 mg
Iron	4 mg

Wheat, Dairy and Egg Free

LENTIL SOUP (1)

Serves 4

500 g brown lentils
(soaked for 2 hours and strained)
2 lt water
2 onions, chopped
1 potato
1 carrot
2 stalks celery
2 tomatoes
2 cloves garlic
½ tsp sea salt

Dice all vegetables. Place in a pot with the lentils and water. Bring to the boil and simmer for 30 minutes

	Per Serve
Protein	24 g
Calcium	70 mg
Iron	7 mg

Wheat, Dairy and Egg Free

LENTIL SOUP (2)

A hearty meal, serve with crusty bread.

Serves 8

2 chopped onions
2 garlic cloves – crushed
1 tsp coriander
1 tsp cumin
1 tsp turmeric
1 dsp curry powder
2 large carrots cubed
2 cup red lentils uncooked
3 large zucchini cut into bite size
1/2 small cauliflower
1 can crushed tomatoes
2 tbs tamari

Saute the onions in a little water.
When soft, add the garlic, then the coriander, cumin, turmeric and curry powder.
Mix through well. Add the lentils and enough water to cover. Cover with lid and simmer for approximately 30 minutes checking to see that there is enough liquid, adding extra water as required.
When lentils are cooked, add the zucchini, carrot, cauliflower, tomatoes and tamari.
Simmer until zucchini and cauliflower are tender.
Check for flavour and add a small amount of Herbamare and extra curry powder,
if required.
Serve with soy yoghurt and chopped fresh coriander.

	Per Serve
Protein	24.5 g
Calcium	131 mg
Iron	5.5 mg

Wheat, Dairy and Egg Free

OATMEAL SOUP

Serves 4

½ cup oatmeal, (for a nutty taste, toast the oats in oven before blending), blend in 6 cups water and add vegetables.
1 leek or onion, sliced
2 cups carrot, diced
1 cup swede, diced
1 cup turnip, diced
2 stalks celery, sliced
**Flavourings as desired - Braggs or
a pinch of Herbamare**
Cook until vegetables are tender

	Per Serve
Protein	1.5 g
Calcium	34 mg
Iron	1 mg

Wheat, Dairy and Egg Free

MISO SOUP BASE

Serves 4

1 stick washed Kombu
1 cup diced carrots
6 cups cold water
1 cup diced cabbage
2 small onions, chopped
1 tbs grated green ginger
1 tbs barley miso
4 spring onions, chopped
1 cup sliced celery

Simmer the Kombu, onions, carrots, cabbage and celery in water for 30 minutes.
Take out the Kombu and chop finely.
Return to pot with miso dissolved in ½ cup warm water and ginger. Mix but don't boil.
Serve with spring onions on top.

	Per Serve
Protein	2 g
Calcium	72 mg
Iron	2.5 mg

Traditional Additions:
1 cup diced tofu
½ cup sliced shiitake mushrooms
½ sheet nori, shredded (add when serving)

	Per Serve
Protein	5 g
Calcium	23 mg
Iron	0.5 mg

Wheat, Dairy and Egg Free

MUSHROOM SOUP

Serves 4

6 cups chopped mushrooms
1 cup chopped onion
1 tbs tamari
1 tsp Herbamare
1 cup soy milk

Optional – plain yoghurt and chopped parsley for serving.

Put all ingredients, except soy milk, in a saucepan and cover with water so that it is approximately 2½ cm above mushrooms.
Cook gently until mushrooms are soft.
Puree and add soy milk.
Reheat but do not boil.
Serve with a dollop of yoghurt and some chopped parsley on top.

	Per Serve
Protein	5 g
Calcium	30 mg
Iron	1.5 mg

Wheat, Dairy and Egg Free

SIMPLE MINESTRONE SOUP

Serves 4

2½ litres water with 4-6 beef cubes dissolved in it.
1 cup diced carrots
1 cup diced celery
1 cup diced tomatoes
1 cup diced green beans
2 cups shell noodles (rice)
½ tsp sea salt

Place all ingredients except noodles in a saucepan and boil for 20 minutes, stirring occasionally. Add noodles for the last 10 minutes. Serve with garlic bread.

	Per Serve
Protein	3 g
Calcium	40 mg
Iron	3 mg

Wheat, Dairy and Egg Free

PARSNIP & LEEK SOUP

Serves 6

1 kg parsnips
2 large leeks
1 large onions
1 large potatoes
1 tsp crushed garlic
2 stalks celery
1½ litres water
½ tsp thyme, oregano, coriander or cumin
Pinch of paprika

Bring water to boil, add vegetables – coarsely chopped.
Then add herbs and spices.
Simmer until cooked, blend, add soy milk if too thick.

	Per Serve
Protein	24 g
Calcium	122 mg
Iron	4 mg
Saturated Fat	5 g

Wheat, Dairy and Egg Free

SPECIAL SPINACH SOUP

Serves 4

1 large bunch spinach
½ litre water
1 medium onion, chopped
2 tbs flour of choice
½ tsp sea salt
1 tbs lemon juice
1 litre water and 2 bouillon cubes
1 hard boiled egg
2 tbs plain yoghurt

Wash spinach and cook 10 minutes in the ½ litre water.

Drain and reserve liquid, adding it to the 1 litre water and cubes.
Saute chopped onion in a little water, add flour and keep stirring.
Gradually pour in the 1½ litres of liquid.
Bring to the boil and simmer 10 minutes.
Chop the spinach very finely and add into the soup along with the lemon juice and sea salt, if needed.
Heat gently.
Serve with a slice of egg and a dollop of yoghurt on top.

	Per Serve
Protein	2 g
Calcium	40 mg
Iron	1 mg
Saturated Fat	1 g

SWEET POTATO SOUP

Serves 6

6 cups diced sweet potato
4 cups water
2 small leeks cleaned and sliced
1 clove garlic
1 tsp lemon juice
1 cup soy milk
Optional – spring onion and yoghurt

Place all ingredients except soy milk in a pan and bring to boil.
reduce heat and cover, simmer for 15 minutes or until vegetables are soft.
Puree soup and add soy milk.
Reheat and serve with a dollop of yoghurt and sprinkle of spring onions.

	Per Serve
Protein	6 g
Calcium	84 mg
Iron	2 mg

Wheat, Dairy and Egg Free

113

TOMATO SOUP

Serves 4

¾ kg ripe tomatoes
2 cups water
1 medium onion
1 tsp Herbamare
1 tsp chopped basil
1 bay leaf
½ tsp honey
2 cups soy milk (optional)

Chop tomatoes and onions, put into a sauce pan with other ingredients except soy milk. Simmer until vegetables are cooked and soft. Puree and add soy milk if a creamy soup is required or more water if thin soup is required. Reheat gently, do not boil as soy milk may curdle.

	Per Serve
Protein	5 g
Calcium	47 mg
Iron	1.5 mg

Wheat, Dairy and Egg Free

SAUCES & DRESSINGS

CURRIED YOGHURT SAUCE

Serves 4

½ cup water
1 onion diced small
1 tsp curry powder
1½-2 cups soy yoghurt
3 tsp corn flour dissolved in ¼ cup cold water

Saute onion in water. Add curry powder. Cook for 3 minutes. Add yoghurt and heat gently, if too thin add corn flour and boil for 1 minute. Pour sauce over hot vegetables and serve with diced marinated tofu.

	Per Serve
Protein	8 g
Calcium	152 mg
Iron	1 mg
Saturated Fat	2.5 g

Wheat, Dairy and Egg Free

MUSHROOM SAUCE

Serves 4

4 cups thinly sliced mushrooms
1 tbs tamari
2 cloves of chopped garlic
1 small sliced onion
1½ cups water

Simmer all together till tender and thicken with 1 tbs cornflour dissolved in ¼ cup water if necessary. Stir until boiling. Boil 1 minute.

	Per Serve
Protein	7 g
Calcium	39 mg
Iron	4.5 mg

Wheat, Dairy and Egg Free

FLAX OIL DRESSING

5 tbs flax seed oil (cold extracted)
1 small clove garlic crushed
½ tsp mustard
3 tbs apple cider vinegar
½ tsp honey

Combine all the ingredients well
(a Bamix works best).
Store in refrigerator.
This is a base dressing recipe.
Contains a good quantity of Omega 3.

To this can be added almost any other flavour
such as:
- chopped sundried tomato and olives
- avocado pureed
- any pureed vegetable or legume
- soy mayonnaise
- any herbs or extra garlic.

	Per Serve
Protein	2.5 g
Calcium	72 mg
Iron	1.5 mg

GOLDEN SAUCE FOR PASTA

Serves 4

2 cups diced carrots
1 cup diced sweet potato
2 cups diced pumpkin
1 cup diced onion
1 tsp crushed garlic
1 tsp Herbamare
2 tsp cumin powder
Optional for serving: spring onion, parsley,
Parmesan cheese

Place all ingredients in a saucepan and cover
with water.
Bring to a boil, then simmer gently for
approximately 30 minutes.
Mash or puree the vegetables and serve over
pasta, sprinkle with a little spring onion, parsley
or Parmesan cheese.

MUSHROOM STROGANOFF SAUCE

Serves 4

1 large onion, diced
½ green capsicum, sliced
1 cup sliced celery
4 cups chopped mushrooms
1 tbs rice flour
1 cup water
1 tbs yeast flakes
¼ cup yoghurt
2 tsp tamari
½ tsp thyme
2 tbs chopped parsley
1 dsp corn flour mixed with cold water to
a thin paste
1 cup diced tofu (optional)

Saute onions in a little water, add celery,
capsicum and mushrooms.
Cook 5 minutes.
Stir in rice flour, add water, yeast flakes
and thyme.
Bring to the boil and simmer for 3 minutes.
Add parsley and thickening and boil for
1 minute.
Remove from heat and stir in yoghurt and
tamari.
Serve over rice or pasta.

	Per Serve
Protein	5.5 g
Calcium	71 mg
Iron	2.5 mg

**Wheat, Dairy and Egg
(if using soy yoghurt)**

MUSTARD SAUCE

Serves 4

1 cup soy mayonnaise
2 tsp popped mustard seeds
(heat gently in a dry pan, shaking well)
1 tsp mustard
2 tbs chopped fresh chives

Combine all ingredients.
Mix well.

	Per Serve
Protein	2 g
Calcium	20 mg
Iron	1 mg
Saturated Fat	4 g

Wheat, Dairy and Egg Free

ONION GRAVY

Serves 4

2 roughly chopped onions
1 tbs mineral bouillon
½ chopped garlic
3 cups water
½ tsp mixed herbs
1 tbs cornflour

Boil all together except cornflour, until onions
are cooked.
Thicken with cornflour blended with a little
cold water.
Boil one minute longer.

PESTO

Handful fresh parsley
Handful fresh basil
2 tbs soy mayonnaise
2 cloves garlic
Dash of lemon juice
Herbamare (to taste)

Blend all ingredients together
(use a food processor or blender) to
a soft paste consistency.

PIZZA SAUCE

2 medium onions, diced
2 x 400 g cans pureed tomatoes (or 1 kg
chopped fresh tomatoes)
1 small can tomato paste
1 tsp basil
1 tsp oregano
2 tsp crushed garlic
2 tbs tamari or 1 tsp Herbamare

Mix all ingredients in a saucepan and boil for
5 minutes to thicken.
Pita breads can be used as a base.
Top with the tomato sauce and any vegetables
of choice, raw, grated or lightly steamed.
Place topped pizza on a greased tray and heat
in oven for 15 minutes at 200°C.

	Per Serve
Protein	6 g
Calcium	115 mg
Iron	1 mg

SALMON SAUCE WITH RICE NOODLES

Serves 4

3 cups rice pasta
1 x 415 g can pink salmon (drain and break up with fork)
1 cup sliced carrots
1 cup sliced red capsicum
½ cup sliced snow peas

Cook rice pasta in boiling water for
8-10 minutes.
Drain and rinse under cold running water and
set aside.
Steam vegetables lightly.
Place a pot of water to boil, when boiling add
pasta, reheat 30 seconds and drain.
Place in bowls, add salmon sauce and then
top with steamed vegetables.

Sauce:

½ litre milk
½ red onion finely chopped
2 tbs plain flour
2 tbs butter
1 tsp Herbamare
2 tbs water
2 tbs chopped parsley

Saute onion in 1 tbs water and 1 tbs butter for
5 minutes. Add the extra butter and the flour.
Cook, stirring for several minutes gradually
pouring in milk stirring constantly to remove
the lumps. Boil for 1 minute.
Add Herbamare and salmon and parsley.

	Per Serve
Protein	28 g
Calcium	320 mg
Iron	3 mg

SATAY SAUCE

Serves 4

3 cups vegetable stock or water
½ cup almonds
½ tsp chopped garlic
1 tsp grated green ginger
1 tsp cider vinegar
1 tbs diced onions
½ tsp curry powder
¼ tsp hot paprika
½ tsp honey
1 tbs low salt tamari
1 tbs cornflour

Saute onions in a little water, add the rest of
the ingredients, except cornfour mix.
Boil for a few minutes, dissolve cornflour in
¼ cup cold water and add.
Mix and boil, adjust seasonings to taste.

SWEET & SOUR SAUCE

1 ½ cups apple cider vinegar
½ cup honey

Simmer together until thin cream consistency
and light golden colour.

TEMPEH PASTA SAUCE

Serves 4

2 cups diced tempeh (unseasoned)
3 cups finely chopped mushrooms
4 spring onions, chopped
1 cup diced tomato
½ cup diced onion
½ tsp chopped garlic
1 dsp miso
1 dsp **Braggs** bouillon
½ cup water
tamari

Simmer tempeh in 2 tbs tamari and 1 cup
water for 10 minutes.
Sauté diced onion in a little water.
Add mushrooms.
Cook for 2 minutes.
Add tomato, garlic and rest of water.
Bring to the boil, stir in miso and spring onions.
Serve over pasta of choice and sprinkle
tempeh on top.

	Per Serve
Protein	11 g
Calcium	64 mg
Iron	3 mg

Wheat, Dairy and Egg Free

WHITE SAUCE

Serves 4

1 cup soy milk
1 cup water
½ tsp hot English mustard
1 tbs soy mayonnaise
1 small onion
2 tsp mineral Bouillon
½ tsp Herbamare
1 tbs cornflour mixed with 3 tbs cold water

Dice onion and saute in a little water.
When transparent add soy milk, water, bouillon,
Herbamare and mustard.
Bring to boil and thicken with cornflour mix.
Boil again for 1 minute.
Whisk in mayonnaise.

YOGHURT AND DILL SAUCE

Serves 4

1 cup soy yoghurt
2 tbs soy mayonnaise
2 tsp crushed dill seed
1 tbs lemon juice

Mix well together and refrigerate.

CAKES

ALLERGY-FREE FRUIT CAKE

¾ cup sultanas
1 cup currants
¾ cup chopped raisins
2 cups water
1 ½ cups cold mashed pumpkin
1 tbs grated lemon rind
¼ cup cold pressed olive oil
1 ½ cups soy flour
1 ½ cups rice flour
3 tsp baking powder
1 ½ tsp cinnamon
¾ tsp nutmeg
2 tbs sugarless apricot jam

Line a deep 20 cm cake tin with 2 sheets of greaseproof paper.
Combine sultanas, currants, raisins and water in a pan, bring to the boil.
Remove from heat, stir in pumpkin, rind and oil.
Cool to room temperature.
Stir sifted flours, baking powder and spices into fruit mixture.
Spread into tin and bake in moderately slow oven for about 1½ hours.
Cover and cool in pan.
Turn out when cold, brush top with warmed sieved jam.

No Saturated Fat
No Added Sugar

Dairy, Egg and Gluten Free

APPLE BARS

½ cup rye flour
½ cup soy compound (not flour)
½ tsp salt skip (baking powder substitute)
½ tsp cinnamon
2 large apples, grated

2 tsp lemon juice
2 tbs honey

Sift together the dry ingredients.
Mix apple, lemon and honey together.
Combine wet and dry ingredients, mix well.
Pour into a greased 20 cm × 20 cm cake pan.
Bake for 20 minutes at 200°C.
Cool and cut.

No Saturated Fat

Wheat, Dairy and Egg Free

APPLE CAKE

Serves approximately 8

4 tsp substitute raising agent or
2 tsp baking powder
225 gm flour – eg. 125 g rice flour + 100 g rye flour or flour of choice
1 tsp cinnamon
1 tsp mixed spice
75 g butter
½ cup honey
3 cups chopped apples
½ cup apple juice

Mix together dry ingredients.
Rub in butter.
Stir in honey, apples and apple juice, mixture should be moist and sticky.
Spread into lightly greased tray.
Bake in oven at 170°C for 20 minutes.
Cool in the tin.

	Whole cake
Calcium	940 mg
Saturated Fat	43 g

Wheat and Egg Free

APPLE FRUIT MUFFINS

1 ½ cups SR flour – spelt or wholemeal
½ cup grated apple
½ cup currants
1 tsp mixed spice
1 egg, beaten
1 dsp lime marmalade or jam of choice
Third of a cup milk or soy milk

Grease 8-10 muffin tins.
Mix all ingredients together and place in pans.
Bake for 20-25 minutes at 180°C.

APRICOT CAKE

2 cups brown SR rice flour
2 cups spelt SR flour or 4 cups altogether of flour of choice
2 cups chopped dried apricots
2 cups chopped raw cashew nuts
½ cup sugar
1 tsp bicarbonate of soda
2 dsp cinnamon
2 tbs butter
2 eggs
2¼ cups water
2 tsp vanilla essence

Place the water and butter in a pan and bring to boiling point.
Meanwhile sift the dry ingredients together and add the apricots and nuts.
Make a well in the centre of dry ingredients and pour in the hot liquid.
Mix just until combined.
Add the beaten eggs and vanilla.
Spoon into a greased paper lined 23 cm cake tin and bake at 180°C for about 1 hour.
Test with a knife blade, if it comes out without mix sticking to it, it is done.

Note: This is a delicious, very firm textured cake that cuts well. The eggs can be omitted but will make the cake texture a little looser.

CHOC CHERRY COOKIES

125 gr butter
1 third of a cup of castor sugar
1 third of a cup of brown sugar
1 egg
1¾ cup self raising flour of choice
¾ cup chopped cherries
¾ cup choc bits

Beat butter, sugar and egg in a bowl with electric beater until light and fluffy.
Add flour, cherries and choc bits.
Place a dessert spoon of the mix onto a greased tray.
Bake in a moderate oven 180° for 12-15 minutes.
Cool on tray.

CORNFLAKE COOKIES

2½ cups cornflakes lightly crushed
130 gr butter
¼ cup castor sugar
1 egg
¾ cup sultanas or currants
1 tsp lemon essence
1 cup self raising flour of choice

Beat butter, sugar and egg until light & fluffy.
Stir in fruit and the flour.
Roll small balls of the mix in the cornflake crumbs, flatten slightly.
Cook on a greased tray in a moderate oven 180° for 12-15 minutes.

APRICOT TOFU SLICE

Base:

1½ cups rolled oats (place in a food processor with knife blade, pulse chop a couple of times to break up the large flakes)
½ cup rice flour
½ cup almond meal
½ cup honey
½ cup wholemeal flour or flour of choice
1 tsp baking powder
125 g unsalted butter, melted

Mix all ingredients well and pat into a greased pan (approx. 18 cm x 24 cm).
Bake for 20 minutes at 160°C.

Filling:

500 g firm tofu
2 cups chopped, dried apricots
¼ cup honey
1 cup soy milk
3 tbs finely grated orange rind

Blend all together well, pour onto base.
Bake at 180°C for 35 minutes.
Cool, then chill, before cutting.

Protein	42 g
Calcium	819 mg
Iron	26 mg

BERRY MUFFINS

Makes 12

2 cups plain flour of choice
4 tsp baking powder substitute or 2 tsp baking powder or 2 cups SR flour
1 cup maple syrup
2 tbs olive oil
2 eggs
¼ cup milk of choice

1 tsp vanilla
1 cup whole berries (blue, cranberry or raspberry)
½ cup chopped pecans

Sift flour and baking powder if used.
In a separate bowl beat together the maple syrup, oil, eggs, milk and vanilla.
Stir dry ingredients into liquid ingredients
Don't over beat and fold in berries and nuts.
Spoon into greased muffin tins.
Bake for 15 minutes at 180°C.

CAROB COOKIES (NO BAKE)

Makes 24

½ cup each honey, butter and milk
3 tbs carob powder or cocoa
½ cup tahini
1 tsp vanilla
½ cup chopped nuts (not peanuts)
3 cups rolled oats, chopped

Combine the butter, honey, milk and carob powder and bring to the boil in a saucepan.
Boil 1 minute, remove from heat, beat in tahini, vanilla, oats and nuts.
Drop in spoonfuls on a greased tray and chill in refrigerator.

CAROB FUDGE

¾ cup soft unsalted butter
½ cup honey
I tsp vanilla
2 tbs water
I cup non-instant powdered milk or soy
compound (not flour)
½ cup carob powder
2 cups chopped nuts of choice

Cream butter and honey, add vanilla and water.
Add carob and milk powders.
Mix at high speed for several minutes.
Stir in nuts, spread in a greased 20 cm x 20 cm
pan, chill, then cut.

Protein	44 g
Calcium	625 mg
Iron	9.5 mg
Saturated Fat	12 g

CHEWY DOUBLE CHOC CHIP COOKIES

½ cup pitted dates
2 tsp vanilla extract
½ tbs baking powder
20 almonds (optional)
I cup fruit juice (apple, berry etc.)
½ cup wholemeal flour
½ cup carob chips
½ cup each oat bran and wheat bran

Preheat oven to 180°C.
Pulse chop the dates and the fruit juice in a
food processor.
Add vanilla and puree for several seconds.
Stir together the bran, flour and baking powder,
then pulse chop them in the processor with
the juice mixture.
Transfer to a medium bowl.
Stir in carob chips, roll in balls (3 cm), press
almond in centre and bake 15 minutes.

DATE LOAF

I cup flour of choice 50/50 wholemeal/rice flour
½ tsp bi-carb soda
2 tsp cinnamon
½ cup each dates and walnuts
25 gm butter
2/3 cup water
Grease and line a loaf tin.
Sift dry ingredients together.
Mix in the dates and nuts.
Heat the water and butter in a saucepan
to nearly boiling.
Quickly but thoroughly mix into
the dry ingredients.
Bake at 180°C for 40 minutes.

Protein	15 g
Calcium	130 mg
Iron	8.5 mg
Saturated Fat	30 g

Egg Free

DRIED APRICOT AND APPLE BARS

I cup dried chopped apricots
I cup dried chopped apples
2 tbs honey
¼ cup powdered milk
Coconut

Mix honey and powdered milk together.
Add fruit and form into balls.
Roll in coconut.
If fruit is too dry, pour warm water over and
then squeeze and drain it off.
Let stand for a while and then roll.

EASTER CAKE

1 cup raisins
2 cups dates roughly chopped
½ cup currants roughly chopped
1 cup fresh bread crumbs
1½ cups ground almonds
¼ cup finely grated orange rind
¼ cup finely grated lemon rind
2 tsp cinnamon
1 tsp mixed spice
1 tbs lemon juice

Pulse-chop all ingredients in a food processor. You may need to do it in two batches, as the mix will pack together.

Almond/Marzipan Paste:

375 g ground almonds
1 large egg white (or 2 small egg whites)
1½ tbs honey
2 tsp lemon juice – or more if needed, to combine
2 tsp brandy (optional)

Mix all ingredients together, using hands if necessary, no longer than needed to combine. Wrap in greaseproof paper and refrigerate until needed.

Place ½ the fruit mix into a lightly greased cake pan. Pat down.
Roll out ½ the almond paste to 12-15 cm and place on top of the mixture in pan.
Add the rest of the fruit mix.
Pat down firmly.
Refrigerate for 2 hours.
Roll out balance of the almond/marzipan paste.
Turn cake out of pan and lay rolled-out marzipan paste on the top and crimp the edges.
Sides of the cake can be coated with melted carob buds or 70% cocoa dark chocolate.
Marzipan top can be decorated with small eggs made from the Easter Egg recipe.

Note: Easter Cake recipe can be made into balls. Roll in a mixture of carob powder and almond meal.

Protein	31 g
Calcium	432 mg
Iron	12 mg

Dairy and Egg Free
Wheat Free
(if using rice breadcrumbs or spelt)

EASTER EGGS

½ cup almond butter
1 cup raisins
½ cup coconut
1 tbs carob powder
1 tsp honey
½ tsp vanilla

Pulse-chop all ingredients in processor until the mixture holds together.
Shape into small eggs and refrigerate until really firm.
Can be coated in melted carob buds or 70% cocoa dark chocolate.
Melt carob buds or chocolate in a bowl over a pot of simmering water.
Dip eggs one at a time and allow to set on greased greaseproof paper

HONEY CARAMELS

I cup honey
I cup evaporated milk
I tsp vanilla essence
3 tbs butter, melted
Pinch salt
I cup chopped nuts

Mix honey and milk, cook stirring to a
firm ball stage.
Stir into butter, nuts vanilla essence.
Pour into buttered square cake pan.
Cool and cut into squares.

———•———

JOHN'S CAKE

1/3 cup brown rice flour
1/3 cup soy flour
1/3 cup corn flour
4 tsp salt skip, baking powder substitute, or 2 tsp
baking powder
2/3 cup sultanas
2/3 cup raisins
2/3 cup chopped apricots or dates
2/3 cup coconut
2 cups, approximately, soy milk

Sift dry ingredients.
Add all other ingredients, and place in a
greased 23 cm cake tin.
Cook at 170°C for approx. 30 minutes.
Better eaten within 48 hours, can get a little
dry as there is no shortening or egg.

Protein	66 g
Calcium	372 mg
Iron	32 mg

———•———

MUESLI SLICE

2½ cups muesli
(break up a little in a food processor)
250 g plain yoghurt
Jam or stewed fruit
I tsp cinnamon
Extra I cup muesli

Combine 2½ cups muesli and yoghurt.
Press into 28 cm x 18 cm tray.
Cover with fruit or spread.
Sprinkle extra cup muesli on top and press
down firmly.
Bake for 30 minutes at 180°C.
Allow to cool in tray for at least 12 hours
before cutting into bars.

Protein	42 g
Calcium	371 mg
Iron	14.5 mg

**Dairy and Egg Free
(if using soy yoghurt)**

———•———

NUTTY FRUIT BARS

Makes 24

1/3 cup honey
1/3 cup raisins
1/3 cup sunflower seeds
¼ cup chopped pitted dates
¼ cup chopped dried apricots
¼ cup raw nuts
I cup hulled sesame seeds

Melt honey in pan and stir in rest of
ingredients.
Mix well and pour into 9" buttered pan.
Allow to dry at room temperature for
3-4 hours.
Cut into bars.

———•———

PINEAPPLE FRUIT CAKE

470 g can crushed pineapple
125 g butter
1/2 cup sugar
500 g dried fruit of choice
1 tsp mixed spice
1 tsp bi-carbonate of soda
1 cup SR flour of choice
1 cup Plain flour of choice
2 eggs

Preheat oven to 180°C.
Line a greased 18 cm cake pan with greased greaseproof paper.
Drain pineapple and put pulp in saucepan with ½ cup of the juice.
Add other ingredients except flour and eggs.
Bring to the boil and simmer 3 minutes.
Cool completely.
Sift flour and beat eggs.
Add to fruit mix.
Place in prepared tin and bake for 1¾ hours at 160°C.

SCONES (Spelt Flour/Savoury)

3 cups spelt flour or flours of choice
5 tsp baking powder substitute or 2½ tsp baking powder (or 3 cups of SR flour).
½ cup plain yoghurt
¼ - ½ cup soy, oat or rice milk
½ tsp Herbamare
¼ tsp chopped rosemary
½ tsp chopped thyme
1 tbs chopped parsley

Sift flour and baking powder into a bowl, add all seasonings.
Make a well in the centre and pour in the yoghurt and milk,
Mix gently to a soft dough; if mix crumbly add more milk. and turn out onto a floured surface.

Pat out to a 3 cm thickness, cut into rounds and place onto a greased oven tray and bake for approximately 15 minutes at 220°C.
Makes 10 scones.
For sweet scones, omit Herbamare and herbs.
Add ¾ cup currants and 1 tablespoon of honey (mixed in with milk and yoghurt).

Protein	24 g
Calcium	141 mg
Iron	2.5 mg

SPICE CAKE

2 cups spelt flour, or flour of choice
4 tsp salt skip (baking powder substitute)
1 tsp cinnamon
½ tsp allspice
1 cup rolled oats, chopped in food processor
½ cup butter
½ cup honey
2 tbs unsulphured blackstrap molasses or golden syrup
2 eggs
1 cup milk of choice

Sift together flour and spices. Add oats.
Cream butter, honey and syrup,
add eggs and milk.
Stir dry ingredients into wet mixture and stir until well mixed.
Bake in a greased 23 cm cake pan for 35 minutes at 200°C.

Protein	130 g
Calcium	380 mg
Iron	60 mg

Wheat Free

RICE BUBBLE BALLS

½ cup honey
1 tsp vanilla essence
½ cup powdered milk (non instant)
½ cup peanut butter
4 cups rice bubbles

Heat honey and remove from heat.
Add powdered milk, peanut butter
and vanilla essence.
Mix thoroughly and pour over
the rice bubbles.
Form into small balls.
Can add ¼ cup carob or choc chips just
before forming balls.

ZUCCHINI COOKIES

¾ cup butter
¾ cup honey
2 eggs
2 cups grated zucchini
2 tsp lemon juice
2 tsp vanilla essence
1 cup spelt flour
1 cup rice flour
2 tsp cinnamon
3 tsp salt skip (baking powder substitute)
or 1½ tsp baking powder
2 cups rolled oats, chopped roughly in food
processor

Cream butter, honey and eggs.
Add zucchini and vanilla.
Sift dry ingredients into liquid ingredients,
stir in rolled oats.
Drop spoonfuls on a greased tray and bake at
200°C for 10 minutes.

TOFU CHEESE CAKE

Serves 10-12

2 cups rolled oats (ground)
½ cup apple juice concentrate
50 g stoned dates, chopped
4 tbs lemon juice
rind of 1 lemon
3 tbs water
350 g packet of firm tofu
150 ml apple juice
1 banana mashed
1 tsp vanilla essence
1 mango peeled and chopped

Lightly grease 18 cm round loose
bottomed cake tin.
Mix together the oats and apple juice
concentrate, press into the base of pan,
bake in 160°C oven for 15 minutes.
Put the chopped dates, lemon juice,
lemon rind and water into a saucepan
and bring to the boil.
Simmer for 5 minutes until the dates are soft,
then mash them roughly.
Place dates in a blender or processor with the
tofu, apple juice, mashed banana and vanilla
essence then process until the mixture is a
thick smooth puree.
Pour the puree into the prepared base.
Bake in a preheated oven 180°C for 30 to 40
minutes until lightly golden.
Leave to cool in the pan then chill
before serving.
Place mango in blender and process until
smooth; serve as a sauce with chilled
cheesecake.

	Per Serve
Protein	8 g
Calcium	72 mg
Iron	1 mg

Wheat, Dairy and Egg Free

DESERTS

APPLE PUDDING

Serves 4

5 large green cooking apples
½ cup sugar
2 tbs SR flour of choice
1½ tbs melted butter
1 cup cold water

Peel, core and slice apples.
Place in ovenproof dish.
Sift flour, add sugar, then mix in melted butter and cold water.
Pour over sliced apples, bake in moderate oven 45 minutes. Serve with custard or cream.

Calcium	22 mg
Saturated Fat	9 g

Egg Free
Gluten Free (if using rice or spelt flour)

BANANA DESSERT

250 g silken tofu
1 medium ripe banana
1 tbs vanilla
½ cup soy milk
3 dsp arrowroot

Place all ingredients in a saucepan and puree with a Bamix.
Place on heat and whisk gently until mixture boils.
Simmer 3-4 minutes, stirring gently.
Pour into serving glasses or bowls.
Decorate with some fresh fruit slices or chopped nuts.
Chill for several hours before serving.
Store in airtight container, otherwise these soft, chewy cookies get hard after 2-3 days as they are made without shortening.

CAROB SAUCE

1 cup carob buds
1 tsp honey
1 cup soy yoghurt

Place carob buds in a stainless steel bowl over a pot half full of boiling water.
Stir around till melted and whisk in honey and soy yoghurt till emulsified.
Keep stirring over the hot water until smooth.

FRUIT BETTY

Serves 4–6

Sliced bread (number depends on size of bowl)
250 g apples
500 g berries of choice, can be a combination
200 g sugar

Peel, core and slice apples thinly.
Combine with the other fruits, add sugar and heat gently in a pan until sugar is dissolved.
Grease pudding basin or mould and cut crusts off enough slices of bread to line the sides and base and to cover the top.
Pack slices close together.
Pour fruit into the bowl and cover top with remaining bread.
Choose a plate to fit directly on top of the pudding, grease the underneath of the plate, ,place on top of the pudding. Bake in the oven for 35 minutes at 180°C.

Note: Spelt grain can be tolerated by most people who have an allergy to gluten.

FRUIT JELLIES

Serves 4–6

1 lt pear or apple juice
2 tbs heaped agar agar or kanten flakes or powder
1 cup raspberries
1 cup blueberries

Place ½ litre juice in a saucepan with the agar agar or kanten, stir and bring to a slow boil.
Boil 5 to 10 minutes until agar agar is dissolved, stirring constantly.
Add the other ½ litre juice and pour into individual bowls, add the berries and allow to set.
Top with yoghurt or whipped cream if desired.

Note:
Agar agar or kanten is a vegetable gelatine.
1 level dsp to a cup of liquid can be used to set any liquid to a jelly. Any fruit or vegetable can be set with this.

¾ cup unsweetened pineapple juice
1 cup water
1 can pineapple pieces
3 tsp agar agar powder

Boil the agar agar in the water stirring occasionally until agar agar dissolves.
Stir in pineapple juice and roughly chop the pineapple pieces.
Add to the agar agar mix as the jelly begins to set.
This basic method can be used with most fruit and juices. 1 tsp agar agar to 1 cup of juice.
Fold in the fruit after the jelly cools a little, otherwise the fruit will sink to the bottom of the container.
Cut oranges in half. Scoop out pulp being careful not to break skin.
Let jelly cool a little before filling the shell with the fruit jelly and allow to set. Cut in half again.

ICE CREAM CHRISTMAS PUDDING

600 mls cream
125 g icing sugar
50 g slivered almonds
1 cup sultanas
50 g glace cherries
50 g candied peel
4 egg whites
1 dsp brandy (optional), or more if desired
1 dsp mixed spice
1 tsp cinnamon
1 tsp nutmeg
1 dsp cocoa powder
2 dsp hot water

Marinate all fruit and spices overnight in brandy. Dissolve cocoa in hot water.
Beat together cream and half the sugar until whipped.
Beat egg whites and remaining sugar until stiff.
Fold egg whites and cream together gently.
Add all other ingredients, combine well.
Pour into 2 litre container or mold and freeze.
Note: A special occasion dessert.
Not particularly nutritious, but enjoy.

ICE CREAM - 1

500 mls grape juice
100 g creamed coconut
3 tbs tahini
2 tbs carob or cocoa powder
1 tsp vanilla essence

Place 1 cup juice, tahini, vanilla essence and carob in a blender.
Place other cup of juice in a pan with the creamed coconut and heat gently until coconut melts.
Pour into the blender with other ingredients and blend at high speed for 3 minutes.
Pour into trays and freeze for 3 to 4 hours.

128

ICE CREAM - 2

6 large ripe bananas; break into 3 or 4 pieces
1 tbs honey
4 tbs soy milk powder (Roberts soy compound,
not flour)
1/3 cup grape juice
½ cup finely chopped dates
1/3 cup cold pressed oil

Place all ingredients in a blender and blend
until smooth.
Place in trays and freeze.

ICE CREAM - 3

3 egg yolks
3 egg whites stiffly beaten
½ cup honey
3 cups yoghurt of choice
1 tsp vanilla

Combine egg yolks, honey, vanilla and yoghurt.
Blend until smooth, fold in beaten whites.
Pour into container and freeze.

JANE'S STEAMED PUDDING

2 cups dried mixed fruit
2 cups homemade breadcrumbs, fresh
6 very ripe bananas mashed

Mix all together.
Place in a pudding basin, cover with greased
greaseproof paper and steam for 1½ - 2 hours.
Or alternatively place on a greased slice tray
and bake in a moderately hot oven.
Can be served as a cake if baked.

OLD FASHIONED LEMON PUDDING

Serves 4

2 tbs sugar
2 tbs butter
2 eggs
Juice and grated rind 1 lemon
3 tbs SR flour of choice
1 cup milk of choice

Cream together butter and sugar, add eggs,
lemon rind and juice.
Add flour and milk alternately.
Bake at 180°C for approximately 30 minutes
until nicely browned on top.

129

SANDWICHES

Some different and nutritious sandwich fillings:

Equal parts cream cheese, almond butter
and shredded lettuce
Cottage cheese and chopped watercress
Cream cheese, dates and cinnamon
Avocado, celery and mayonnaise
Cottage cheese, and grated carrot
Cream cheese, few olives and celery
Mashed banana and almond or cashew butter
Mashed banana, honey and coconut
Tuna, shredded lettuce and mayonnaise
Scrambled egg with mayonnaise
Cream cheese, sultanas and shredded lettuce
Mashed corn with alfalfa, lettuce
and mayonnaise to bind
Mashed baked beans with lettuce

Bread cases:

A change from sandwiches or dry biscuits.

Bread cases are easy to make and add variety
in light lunches or snack foods.

Any required number of bread slices.

Remove crusts from bread, brush one side
with a little melted butter and press buttered
side down, into muffin tins or patty tins. Brush
the inside of the cases with melted butter,
bake in a hot oven, 220°C until crisp and
golden brown (these keep well in an airtight
container). These can be filled with any type of
mixture, salad tidbits, hot creamy food or even
fruit and yoghurt.

SNACK FOODS

EASY DIPPING CHIPS

Sorj or mountain bread

Cut sheets of bread into squares or diamonds
with scissors.
For a different taste you can brush sheets
with tamari before cutting.
Spread out on a baking tray and dry in
the oven until crisp.
Will keep in a sealed jar for several weeks.

FROZEN FRUIT TREATS

1 block carob or chocolate
bananas, grapes or strawberries

Melt carob or chocolate in a bowl over a pot
of boiling water.
Dip pieces of banana, grapes or strawberries in
the melted carob or chocolate.
Place on a greased plate until set.
Remove from plate to a tray suitable to go
into the freezer and freeze.

Note: A nice treat on a hot day.
Many fruits are suitable to thread onto
wooden skewers and freeze. Large grapes
are good for this. Other fruits can be cut to
appropriate size and threaded on skewers.
This is easy for older children to eat but it is
not a suitable way to serve fruit
to small children.
Better fresh and to be served from a bowl
with a spoon.

FROZEN YOGHURT TREATS

Makes 6 popsicles or 10-12 ice blocks

Apple:
1 cup plain yoghurt
1 cup stewed apple
1 tbs honey

Combine and freeze.

Banana:
2 medium bananas
1 cup plain yoghurt
1 tsp lemon juice

Mash bananas with lemon juice.
Stir in yoghurt and freeze.

Banana & Carob
2 medium bananas
1 cup plain yoghurt
1 tsp lemon juice
2 tbs carob powder

Mash bananas with lemon juice.
Mix yoghurt and carob.
Combine and freeze.

Peach:
2 large ripe peaches
1 cup plain yoghurt
1 tsp lemon juice

Puree peaches and lemon juice.
Stir in yoghurt.
Combine and freeze.

Berry:
2 cups fresh or frozen berries
1 tbs honey
1 cup plain yoghurt

Puree berries and honey.
Stir in yoghurt and freeze.

VEGETABLE STICKS IN PASTRY

Vegetables of choice
2 sheets filo pastry

Cut vegetables
(i.e. carrots, sweet potato, parsnip or potato)
into finger sized pieces,
1 cm x 3 cm x 7 or 8 cm.
Steam until just tender.
Cut two sheets of filo pastry into
7 or 8 cm squares.
Lay a piece of vegetable on each square
diagonally.

Sprinkle with Herbamare and roll up, leaving
each end open to expose the tip
of the vegetable.

Place on a lightly greased oven tray and bake
until golden for about 10-18 minutes in a
moderate oven.

Can brush with a little egg yolk and sprinkle
with seeds of choice before cooking.

BREAD

BREAD & SAVOURY FOCACCIA

4 cups flour – made up of 3 cups spelt flour
and 1 cup organic unbleached white
2 tbs olive oil
1 tbs honey
2 tsp yeast (dried granulated)
2 tsp bread improver
4-5 cups warm water
(sundried tomatoes & olives needed if making
focaccia)

Add yeast and improver to flours.
In a separate bowl, mix honey, olive oil and
warm water.
Add the liquid to the flour and mix through.
Put dough on a bench and knead thoroughly.
Place back into floured bowl and cover
with a damp cloth.
Place in a warm spot and let rise to
double the size.
Take dough from bowl and punch down.
Knead thoroughly and place in a greased
bread tin, or make into rolls.
Cover with damp cloth and let rise again.
Bake in a hot oven until hollow sounding
when tapped! Cool.

To make Focaccia:

Add chopped sundried tomatoes and chopped
olives to the flour mix before adding the liquid.
After the first rising, knead and cut into 4 or
smaller as required.
Roll out to a round and place on an oven tray.
Cover with a damp cloth and allow to rise.
Bake in a hot oven 200°C (about 15 minutes).

SPELT FLOUR BREAD

6 cups spelt flour
2 cups unbleached white or wholemeal flour
1½ tbs dry yeast or 2 oz fresh yeast
3 tsp honey
1 litre water – very warm
1 tbs cold pressed olive oil

Mix ¾ of the dry ingredients together.
Pour in ¾ of the liquid and all the honey.
Mix well.
Add the remaining flours and liquid, mix well,
then let the mixture rest until it doubles in size.
When doubled, remove from bowl onto a
floured surface and knead for 8-10 minutes.
Divide the dough in half and put into two
700 gram bread tins.
Spray with water and allow to
double in size again.
Bake at 220°C for 30 minutes.

	Per Serve
Protein	107 g
Calcium	54 mg
Iron	2.5 mg

WALNUT CORNBREAD

1 cup polenta
1 cup wholemeal or spelt flour
1 tbs baking powder
1 tsp bicarbonate soda
1 tsp cinnamon
1½ cups chopped walnuts
3 bananas
2 tbs honey
2 tsp vanilla essence
½ cup soy milk
¼ cup melted butter or olive oil

Place soy milk, butter, honey, vanilla, essence and 2 bananas in a food processor, process until smooth.
Add the sifted dry ingredients, pulse chop until just blended.
Transfer to a bowl and stir in the walnuts and the one sliced banana.
Pour into a greased pan and bake at 180°C for approximately 50 minutes.

	Per Serve
Protein	51 g
Calcium	248 mg
Iron	13.5 mg

PANCAKES

2 cups wholemeal flour
2 cups water
½ tsp sea salt
1 tsp oil

Combine ingredients in a bowl, whipping by hand . Allow to stand for at least 1 hour.
Heat a frypan greased with a little oil.
Pour in one sixth of the mixture.
Cover and cook for 5 minutes.
Turnover and cook other side for 5 minutes.
Serve with spread or topping of choice.

FLAKEY PIE CRUST

3 cups wholemeal or spelt flour
2 tbs oil - 1 tsp liquid lecithin
½ tsp sea salt
Two thirds of a cup of hot water

Pre-heat the oven to 250°C.
Combine dry ingredients.
Rub in oil and lecithin.
Add hot water slowly.
Roll into a ball and cut in half.
Roll out 1 piece and line a greased pie plate, add filling, roll out other half and place on top.
Prick with a fork and flute the edges.
Bake for 40 to 50 minutes.

DRINKS

ALMOND & HONEY DRINK

¼ cup almonds
2 tsp honey
I cup water

Whiz for a few minutes in a blender.

———•———

HOMEMADE LEMONADE

2 cups lemon juice
½ cup apple juice concentrate

Use as a cordial. I tbs per glass.
Top up with ice blocks and mineral water.
This is still delicious when only water is used to
fill the glass.

———•———

LEMON & HONEY DRINK

Mix the juice of I lemon
I tsp honey
I chopped mint leaf
2 cups water

———•———

SMOOTHIES

Serves 2

I ½ cup milk of choice
2 tbs yoghurt (dairy or soy)
4 chopped dates
½ ripe banana or 4 strawberries
½ tsp vanilla or I dsp carob or cocoa powder

Blend ingredients until smooth.

———•———

STRAWBERRY SHAKE

Serves 3

I cup strawberries
2 tbs apple juice concentrate
2 cups milk of choice
½ cup yoghurt
I tsp honey

Puree and blend until smooth.

———•———

HOMEMADE SOY MILK

225 g soy beans
1.25 litres water
2 tsp honey
I tsp kelp powder or I tsp tamari

Soak the beans for 48 hours.
Drain off and replace the water
every 12 hours.
Drain after 48 hours and grind the beans
to a fine meal in a food processor.
Place the meal in a cheesecloth bag, tie the top.
Place the bag in a bowl of 1.25 litres of luke
warm water.
Move the bag around in the water with your
hands, use a "kneading" motion.
Do this for 10 minutes and then squeeze all
the liquid from the bag.
The milk can then be seasoned with the honey,
the kelp or the tamari. Store in the refrigerator.
Note: Approximate nutrients for 5 cups of
milk.

	Per Serve
Protein	140 g
Calcium	470 mg
Iron	10 mg

Wheat, Dairy and Egg Free

———•———

Useful weights and measures

One cup of Dry Weight in ....

Almonds	equals 200 g
Apricots	equals 200 g
Barley	equals 150 g
Beans	equals 200 g
Brown Rice	equals 200
Buckwheat	equals 250 g
Carob Buds	equals 150 g
Carob Powder	equals 100 g
Chick Peas	equals 150 g
Coconut	equals 100 g
Couscous	equals 150 g
Currants	equals 125 g
Dates	equals 150 g
Flour Rice	equals 150 g
Flour Soy	equals 100 g
Flour W/meal	equals 150 g
Great North Beans	equals 200 g
Lentils	equals 250 g
Lima Beans	equals 150 g
Millet	equals 250 g
Oat Bran	equals 100 g
Polenta	equals 200 g
Raisins	equals 150 g
Semolina	equals 200 g
Soy Comp	equals 100 g
Split Peas	equals 150 g
Sultanas	equals 150 g
Unproc. Bran	equals 100 g
Wild Rice	equals 200 g

Liquid Measures

Millilitres	Cups and Spoons
5 ml	1 Teaspoon (tsp)
20 ml	1 Tablespoon (tbs)
250 ml	1 cup
600 ml	2 ½ cups
1 litre	4 cups

Weight equivalents

Metric	Imperial
30 g	1 oz
100 g	3½ oz
500 g	16 oz
1000 g	2.2 lbs

Oven Temperatures

Slow	150°C
Moderate	180°C
Hot	200 - 210°C
Very Hot	230°C

Complementary Therapies and Remedies

Learning about and using proven Natural and Complementary Therapies can make a big difference to the dietary, physical, emotional and psychological health of children.
Some suggestions and explanations on how to deal with stressful situations are offered by qualified and professional mainstream and Natural Therapists.

Traditional Chinese Medicine (TCM) - Paediatrics.

Brief History
Traditional Chinese Medicine (TCM) as a rule does not harbour specialisation. Almost every traditionally trained TCM practitioner is able to diagnose and treat any given complaint, without specialist knowledge. As usual there are exceptions. Paediatrics is one of those exceptions.

Chao Yuan Fang (550 – 630 AD) is remembered for his suggestion that active care for children is required. He suggests that children are weak in their qi (energy) and blood. Spoiling or pampering children he considered to be bad for their health, and physical exercise increased intelligence and adaptive capacity. This is still acknowledged today in the popular phrase, "a child should know 30% hunger and 30% cold."
Later, *Qian Yi* (1032 – 1113 AD) who has been considered the founder of Chinese Paediatrics, took this and a lot of other previous material on children, and codified it into one book called the Xiao Er Yao Zheng Zhi Jue.
This book postulated that most children are constitutionally hot and fever prone, and need to be cooled and sedated.

He argued that all therapies should be gentle, and he used sweet and cold herbs as well as diet therapy. He also studied in great depth the relationship of the spleen and stomach in regard to childhood illnesses.

A later doctor, *Chen Wen Zhong* (1241 AD) established the school of using warm and tonifying herbs. He suggested, "Things that grow in the shade, do not grow strongly". He also contributed the thought that most childhood diseases are genetic, and that environment is only a secondary factor. Additionally, he warned that children should always keep their abdomen, back and feet warm. This will help to prevent injury to their qi, yang, spleen and kidneys.

Wan Quan stressed diet and regulating the temperature of children. He especially warned against overheating. One of his major contributions was to suggest to parents that their conduct at conception would determine the genetic makeup of the potential child, and therefore the childhood diseases as well. He said "tonify the energy, have strong stamina, avoid aphrodisiacs, and hold good emotions in your heart during intercourse". He also listed the three main causes of illness that he found in children: "Yang excess and yin deficiency, liver strong and spleen weak, and heart strong and kidney/lung weak".

Chen Fu Zheng in his book **You you ji cheng** (Complete work on Paediatrics –1750 AD) was the first to discuss the diagnostic method of testing the index finger for a blue vein. This vein can indicate the depth of the disease and how easily it can be cured. He also championed the use of simple herbal formulas and simple diagnostics for children. So for a distillation and simplification of the complex TCM patterns that have been handed down to us from history, we will look at the three main organs active in children; the lungs, the spleen and the kidneys and their common pathologies.

Taking these organs one at a time, we shall quickly explore each of them and examine how they affect a child's health.

Main organs (TCM)

Lungs

Lungs have an energetic life that begins just after birth, at the first breath. The lung's energy has the responsibility of clearing internal passageways as well as expelling waste and disease. It exercises energetic control over the skin, the hair and the large intestine.
As the immature lung develops, so does the large intestine, and baby's ability to move its bowels becomes stronger, so solid food can be introduced. As the lung progresses in its maturity, the skin becomes less translucent. The immune system strengthens and does not depend as much on the immunity that comes from mother's milk. Also hair grows. Often a baby will have some hair at birth, which is a product of mother's lung energy, transferred to baby, but this growth quickly fades, and it is only when baby's lung solidifies that the hair will again begin to grow.

Emotionally, the lungs control self-esteem and confidence. The volume of the voice and the child's belief in their personal worth can therefore assess the strength of the lungs' energy. So the quiet voice will denote low lung energy and usually, poor self esteem. Those children who speak loudly, and take no regard of who hears them will generally be assessed as having sound lung energy. It is noteworthy that a child will increase the volume of its voice when trying to have its opinion heard, for example, during an argument with a sibling. Yet if they are confident in their position, they will usually remain at a normal, yet robust level. When we discuss the physical manifestations of the lungs we usually refer to the lung system, which comprises the lungs, the bronchia, the throat, the sinuses, the eustachian tubes, the nose and the skin. So when the lungs are sick,

or under attack, there will be dry skin, rashes, cough, fevers, sneezing, and painful sinuses and ears. Due to the fact that lungs' energy and physical nature are outward moving, the ability of the lungs to expel breath can be compromised, as can the ability of the colon to expel stools. So weak lungs can result in constipation and the type of asthma where it is difficult to breathe out.
(Breathing in asthma - refer kidneys).

Spleen

The spleen is fragile in children and generally only a little better in adults. Spleen energy is in charge of transporting and transforming food into energy. It has the energetic control over the muscles, stomach and intestines. Initially a baby has very poor muscle tone, and little control over food processing. When the food is processed poorly it creates phlegm. So goes the saying in TCM "Children are little balls of phlegm". As the spleen strengthens so do the muscles and baby begins to roll, then crawl and eventually walk.

Emotionally the spleen is associated with cognition. The ideas and brainpower of the child will rise and fall with the stages of the spleen. As muscle tone is also associated with the spleen, exercise will assist the development of the intellect, though over-exercise will retard it. It has been well acknowledged at secondary school level that students who play sport appear to achieve more in their academic pursuits.

The main physical symptoms derived from a weak spleen will be excess phlegm, a lack of energy and a lack of memory/or ability to absorb new information. Psychologically it may also cause obsessive behaviour. Obesity is usually considered a spleen weakness in children, though not always in adults. Because the spleen is integrally linked to the stomach, any food allergies, intolerances, nausea or vomiting can be attributed to the spleen's inability to regulate the stomach.

Kidneys

In children, kidneys work hard. From the time of conception they are energetically in charge of constructing the actual body, as determined by the genetic blueprint. For the entire life of a person it is the kidneys that first build and later repair the body. Any damage that must be repaired, whether physical or emotional will require kidney energy. As children are usually full of kidney energy, they typically repair very well. As we grow older, that repair function becomes less competent. In simple terms, this leads to poor repairs, aging, and eventually death. Small scratches, burns and tears to a child's skin can repair so well that they scarcely leave a scar, yet the same injury to an adult will often leave a significant blemish. Any developmental problems, whether physical, mental or emotional, will usually stem from a weak kidney.

The emotion associated with kidneys is fear. When the kidney energy is full, and has little to do, the individual will appear to be fearless and cavalier, as in the case of some older teenagers whose bodies are fully formed. With younger children, their kidneys are busy building their bodies and they tend to suffer fear almost all of the time. This is especially true when they are going through a growth spurt. The bones are growing faster than normal and the kidneys are expending most of their available energy to build the growing bones. It is at these times when children are at their most vulnerable in terms of the development of phobias that may haunt them in later life. As the body of the child enters adolescence, the growth of the body slows down and therefore kidney energy appears to increase at this time. Kidney in adulthood takes on a new function – sex. Hence, teenagers develop an interest shortly after their own bodies reach a certain stage of completion. It is said that the natural progression is for a teenager to look at building another body, once their own is complete. Kidney energy is a powerful force. In some cases, the innate drive to create and build, if subverted, turns to self-destructive tendencies. From a Chinese psychology point of view, this is interpreted as a subconscious desire to do self-harm in order to employ the repair function of kidney.

For many children 'breathing in' asthma is a serious issue that is kidney based. By puberty, the asthma will usually alleviate once the body is strong and kidney has less building to do. Other physical symptoms that relate to weak kidneys will manifest in the form of developmental problems or bone abnormalities.

Therapies (TCM)

Herbs

Herbal medicine has always been well thought of by the TCM historical doctors. *Qian Yi* was the one who first began using *Liu wei di huang wan* formula for children, and this formula is still used for children today. He also acknowledged that children have a poor digestive system, and he combined many of his herbal formulas into pills. By using pills a child's stomach will be able to process the herbs more fully.

Food

Chen Wen Zhong stated, "Children should eat warm, soft and small amounts. If they eat cold, hard and excessive amounts this will lead to disease". This can be seen in the way babies can eat and digest gooey, mushy food, especially if warm, yet cannot deal with high flavour foods. Once children are old enough to eat like adults, they are generally expected to eat what adults eat. This can be an error. It is better to allow taste and stomach ability to mature gradually from warm, soft and small to cold, hard and large.

Tui Na / Baby Massage

The advantage with this type of therapy is that it can be easily taught to the parents, who can administer it daily, without the cost or inconvenience of attending the therapist.

The downside is that it is generally only effective up to the age of four or five.

Acupuncture / Laser

There are many therapists who needle children. This therapy can be beneficial, but may on occasions be too strong. Laser can be a good substitute. Due to the fact that children's meridians run close to the skin, that their skin tends to be more translucent than adults and they have smaller circumference wrists and ankles than adults, laser can generally reach the points easily, with no discomfort to the child.

Upbringing

An adult's self discipline is based and patterned on parental discipline. If you want your child to grow up to be a disciplined adult, discipline them as a child. In TCM, a child who has had a balanced upbringing has a strong heart, heart being heart/mind in Eastern terms. This leads to an adult who, when faced with a life stress, can sit for a moment in deep thought (heart) and discern the most suitable organ to employ to deal with the stress – kidney/fearlessness, lung/confidence, stomach/single-mindedness, liver/fight or flight, etc. and will choose an appropriate response, rather than an habitual one.

Dr Warwick Poon

Cert. B.S.(Ins), Dip.Ac. Cert.O.M., Cert.H.S. Cert.P.P.T., Cert.C.H., A.A.C.M.A, A.A.I.I.

Homoeopathy

Homoeopathy is a complete system of natural medicine developed by German physician, Dr Samuel Hahnemann. The underlying premise is that "like cures like". He found that many substances, when administered to healthy people, could produce symptoms similar to those experienced by sick people.

By using small, especially prepared doses of these substances, illnesses could be cured.

Homoeopathy is non-toxic and non-addictive, is safe for everyone to use and it is acknowledged by the World Health Organization. It takes into account a person's total set of physical, emotional and mental symptoms underlying the tendencies and predispositions when determining a possible cure. It acts as a catalyst in stimulating and strengthening the patient's immune system.

In children, Homoeopathy can be used to treat:

Allergies, asthma, acne, anxiety, Attention Deficit Disorder
Bedwetting, bronchitis, boils
Colic, coughs, colds, croup, constipation
Dermatitis, diarrhoea
Eczema, earache
Fever, flu, flatulence
Gastric problems, ganglions, growing pains
Hives, headache, hay fever, hiccough, hernia
Insomnia, impetigo
Jaundice
Kidney and bladder problems
Lice, laziness, lethargy
Mumps, measles
Nausea, nappy rash, nosebleeds
Otitis Media – acute and chronic
Pimples, psoriasis
Quinsey
Rashes, reflux, ringworm, restlessness
Snuffles, sinusitis, skin, sleeping problems, sore throats
Tantrums, teething, tonsillitis
Upset stomachs, urticaria
Viral infections, vitiligo
Wakefulness, warts, whooping cough, worms, weakness
Xenopthalmia, xanthoderma
Yeast allergies
Zigzags in vision

Suzy Quaife

N.D., DIP. Homeopathy, Member A.H.A, A.T.M.S, A.R.O.H

139

Voice Therapy

Each person begins life with a perfect vocal instrument, in perfect working order, with a delight in spontaneous song and no inhibitions about their individual sound. This can be seen in any new born baby, who exhibits a close connection with sound from the moment of birth, with screams and gurgles covering a vast range, and with young children playing, laughing and singing in the kindergarten playground. But from an early age we begin to struggle, losing touch with sound, caused by physical or psychological injury, as well as social pressure.

The close connection between voice and emotions begins to tangle, the untangling of which is so important that ancient cultures consider vocal work to be a major task of adult life, recognising voice in its important role as a reflection of our personality, a 'mirror of the soul', and a 'repository of ancient wisdom'. That connection between voice, emotion and personality is also seen in our own language in word personality, believed to have derived from the Latin 'persona,' originally meaning the mouthpiece of the mask used by actors (per sona: the sound of the voice passes through), while the term psyche was derived from an older Greek term, psychein, which meant 'to breathe' or 'to blow', the act of which is inextricably linked with making sound.

However, in western culture today, voice has become an area that is undervalued or ignored. Teachers, parents and peers tie knots in vocal identity and vocal damage is often left untended, leaving untold personal difficulties for the voice user to express themselves effectively. Re-addressing that imbalance and working practically on voice, begins with helping children become aware of their breath, feeling proud of their ability to play with spontaneous song and building positive reinforcement of their personal sound and ability to take healthy vocal risk.

For the adult this becomes an awakening of our personal coherence with 'self' and 'other', holding together the connections between body, voice and words and experiencing them through the fullest spectrum of awareness, refining perceptual, kinaesthetic, proprioceptive and interoceptive sensitivity that supports homeostasis and self expression.

The more children are allowed to practically come in touch with a realm of thinking, knowing and being, which is complex, deep and important, something more closely in touch with that ancient wisdom, the more chance they have of not losing that capability through their adult life.

Louise Mahler
BE Com, B Music, Grad Dip Music
Master Applied SC

Other Important Therapies

Meditation
Meditation is connecting to God's frequency, the original source of energy and love in the universe. By freeing your mind for a short while every day you build an irreversible bridge that connects God's vibration with your soul. This conscious dedication to increasing your wellbeing will fill you with peace. The goal of meditation is to achieve a clear awareness of our reality. Clearing our mind, relaxing our body and making ourselves more mentally alert can promote health and harmony within.

Massage Promotes Wellness
Through massage, the lymph system becomes stimulated to cleanse the blood through its elaborate filtration system. It relaxes and rebalances the energy flow of the body.

Shiatsu

Probably originally based on our natural instinct to rub or press on a sore or sluggish part of the body, Shiatsu has been researched and scientifically systematized and improved to become a therapeutic method of carefully judged pressure applied to specific points on our body. It eliminates fatigue and stimulates our body's natural self-healing abilities.

Reflexology

Reflexology is the practice of applying pressure to certain points on the feet and hands, which stimulates corresponding body organs, thus improving circulation and relaxing the body. The simple 'hands on' approach is also a unique opportunity to further the bond with your child while applying a natural solution to a health problem.

Chiropractic

Chiropractic works on the relationship between the spine and nervous system. When our vertebrae are misaligned, they can affect the nerves' ability to supply the correct amount of energy needed to function properly.

Acupuncture

Acupuncture is the technique of stimulating points on the body surface by inserting needles and then applying fingertip pressure or heat, harmonizing our energy or vital force via our body meridians. Acupuncture works exceptionally well in the relief of pain and the elevation of our moods from depression to optimism.

Bach Flower Remedies

Discovered by Dr Edward Bach, the original 38 Bach Flower Remedies are prepared from the flowers of wild English plants. They work on the various negative mental/emotional states, which can cause disease. Remedies have since been prepared from flowers of other countries. They're easily administered to young children and babies, by adding to water, but also as lotion, compress or added to a bath.

Iridology

Used to diagnose body health (past, present and future), iridology interprets colours, lesions and fibres of the iris, which are an extension of our central nervous system.

Biochemic Cell Salts (Tissue Salts)

Biochemic cell salts - or tissue salts - are inorganic mineral substances found in the human body as well as in the earth and soil. If we become deficient in these, disease may follow. The finely prepared particles are used in very small quantities to make up for these deficiencies and are easily absorbed into our blood, tissues and cells.

Herbal Medicine

Many traditional herbal remedies have been handed down from one generation to the next and are extremely useful in preventing and healing illness without the harmful side effects of drugs.

Colour Therapy

Used for centuries, colour therapy is based on the relationship of our body organs and emotions with colour and its effects on our bodily processes and moods. For example, blue calms and red arouses aggression.

Aromatherapy

Aromatherapy is an ancient healing and medicinal practice of using plant and flower essences to increase one's wellbeing. Essential oils are extracted from plants and used to stimulate the body's function via the olfactory sense of smell. The oil is heated in water and then inhaled. Some examples are lavender and chamomile to soothe; eucalyptus and fennel to decongest; and rosemary and peppermint to energise.

Pain Management
In Children

History

It is hard to imagine that 25 years ago babies were having major surgery without pain-relieving drugs. It was thought that a baby's nervous system was immature and therefore not developed enough to register pain signals. In fact we now know that babies feel more pain because the brain and nervous system registers the pain signals, but has not yet learned how to turn them down. Fortunately there has been a boom in the scientific study of pain in the last 20 years, which has challenged some of these myths about pain in children that have been responsible for a tendency to under-treat it.

The experience of pain

Untreated pain can cause anxiety, irritability, depression, acting up and exhaustion. Repeated painful experiences lead to feelings of helplessness and fear of further medical treatment, and alter the development of the nervous system, by lowering the threshold to painful stimuli. Significant childhood pain may contribute to chronic pain later on.

We all want to avoid pain. Parents say that watching their child in pain and feeling that there is nothing they can do to help is the hardest thing. Yet pain does have a purpose. Acute short lived pain lets us know that something is wrong in our body - a warning that we've touched something hot and need to remove our hand or that our gut is inflamed and needs a different diet today, or maybe the heartache of grief when a loved pet dies. Children have to learn to interpret different pain signals and determine the best ways for them to find relief. This is one of the tasks of growing up.

Chronic pain (lasting longer than 3 months) tends to have persisted long beyond its initial protective and informative function. It is often nearly constant and consequently becomes part of the child's life with little hope that it will ever go away, and because chronic pain changes the way the pain system works, it often leads to more pain. The comprehensive treatment and therapy that is required to help children and their families cope with chronic pain is beyond the scope of this article but has been thoroughly dealt with in a recent book called "Conquering Your Child's Chronic Pain. A Pediatrician's Guide for Reclaiming a Normal Childhood" by Dr Lonnie Zeltzer, published by Harper Collins 2005.

Interaction of mind and body

The belief that there are two separate kinds of pain – physical and emotional – is also a misconception. An example is when a child is frightened of having a needle and he or she is told "It's only a needle, it shouldn't hurt". This statement is not taking into account the large anxiety component for this child – maybe it took several attempts last time to get a needle in the vein and the child thought the pain was never going to stop. Anxiety increases pain. The good news is that just as anxiety increases pain, relaxation and other psychological interventions can decrease pain.

As Leora Kuttner writes "In every pain situation, however minor or severe, the interplay of our thoughts, beliefs, emotions and attitudes with the sensations occurring in our bodies creates the experience of pain. This same interaction of mind and body enables us to increase or decrease pain sensations. However young a child is, with a plan and attention to the child's needs, pain can be eased or altered."

Crucial role of parents

It is important that parents recognize their role in this process, and that children understand that they too can help the pain go away. In other words, they can be active participants rather than passive victims.

Parents spontaneously treat their child's pain with a hug, a kiss, a song, or a story, and children find their parents' presence reassuring and want them with them. Examine your own beliefs around pain, and its treatment.

What did you learn about pain from your childhood experiences? Is this what you want for your child?

When your child is in pain it is important to acknowledge his or her pain experience, and neither minimize or deny it. Inform the child what is happening in his or her body, and make physical contact with the child in any way that feels best for you both. Start to use any techniques your child has learned to help pain go away, such as breathing, blowing bubbles, using imagery and relaxation, or listening to a favourite song or story together with medication and physical techniques if appropriate. If possible remain with the child until the pain is under control. Keep your own anxiety under control, since children are like sponges and soak up any tension.

Responding inconsistently, such as fussing over a child one time and then almost ignoring the child next time is unhelpful and can lead to pain behaviour that is misleading. Withdrawing or responding with irritation will not encourage the child to deal effectively with pain. Use language that inspires courage and coping and gives hope that the pain will get better. The first words your child hears after feeling pain will make a difference to whether they cope or worry.

Helping your child through medical procedures.

Children fall and hurt themselves and may need stitches or a plaster, they have regular immunizations and visits to the dentist. Some children struggle with illness and hospital treatment. For years the "get-it-over-with" approach has predominated, and parents have gone along with this, sometimes against their

better judgement. Now the focus is on the needs of the child and family and the goal is avoidance of fear of a subsequent procedure. It is helpful to think of it in stages – before, during and after.

Preparation
Provide your child with simple accurate information in a calm non-emotional manner so they can prepare themselves. Plan and practice strategies well before the procedure. For young children playing or acting out the procedure can be helpful, have a medical kit in the toy box. A local anaesthetic cream can be applied to an area where there is no broken skin, for example for a blood test, an hour in advance, which will help make the area numb. This works best in combination with other techniques described below. Health professionals can also help children develop and expand what works for them, encourage and coach parents to further develop their natural role in this process and invite everyone to be active members of the team. Assess the situation and advocate for your child if necessary. What works for your child may be different from what works for you, or the other adults involved. You may need to switch techniques eg. from distraction to blowing as a needle is inserted.

Relaxation
May be helpful before and during a procedure: blowing away the pain, letting the body go floppy like a rag doll, listening to music or a favourite story. Remain calm so you can support your child. What works for you, may not be what works for your child.

Distraction
Engaging children in age-appropriate activities before and during the procedure that provide a positive focus and divert attention from the negative focus. Blowing bubbles, windmills, pop-up books, toys, other distracting objects, watching a video, singing a song, talking about something you know will capture their

imagination eg. birthday parties, pets.

As children get older they move from needing an external focus, to becoming more internally absorbed using their minds, such as imagining their favourite sport or activity, or creating images that block the pain signals.

It is important to have your child's attention before the procedure.

Holding your child.

If possible, it can be very supportive for your child to have you hold them during a procedure in a positive comforting way. Parents should never be used for negative restraint, indeed it is only in emergencies that a child can be physically restrained for safety. A hospital in USA has popularized a way of holding children during procedures called "positioning for comfort". The main features are allowing the child to be as upright as possible, because children do not like lying down after the age of about 6 months, and using distraction. So a toddler having an immunisation would in effect be having a hug sitting facing the parent on the lap, with the head turned to look at a pop up book for example, in the opposite direction to the limb having the injection. The idea is not to trick the child, but to show them how they need not be bothered by the potentially painful stimulus when they feel secure and focused elsewhere.

Techniques for babies

For babies, rocking, singing, soothing music, holding, gentle massage can reduce the pain experience. Breast feeding your baby during a procedure will provide a familiar comforting focus. To help babies and young children in hospital, who may not have access to a breast, studies have shown the benefit of sucrose on a dummy for reducing pain during procedures. The dose is up to 0.5 ml of 25% sucrose solution. Obviously this is only recommended as a once off at the time of the painful procedure.

Positive helpful self-statements

Coaching older children to use simple statements that encourage and praise themselves "I can do this," "It will be over soon," "Stay calm".

Language of adults

Studies have shown that criticising, apologising, or bargaining with your child is likely to increase distress. Even reassuring statements eg. "I know it's hard or "it'll be all right" are also likely to increase distress. Coping is promoted by talking about things other than the procedure at the time it is happening, praising your child's coping skills and reminding them to use whatever behaviours you have both found helpful such as "breathe" or "blow away the hurt". Give your child some control, for example give them a choice where to sit for a procedure, or what finger to use for a blood test. It is not usually helpful to allow a child to decide when to start a procedure, because this increases anticipatory anxiety.

Afterwards

When you talk about the procedure, focus your child's attention on their helpful coping efforts "It was really good how you looked at the book while you had your treatment". This will help promote a sense of mastery and achievement. Encourage a return to normal pleasant conversation and activities as appropriate and don't focus on the next procedure till nearer the time. Then practice and refine the coping skills which your child used to cope with earlier procedures.

Summary

In conclusion, parents have a crucial role in helping their children learn to cope with pain from whatever cause. The pain of medical procedures serves no useful purpose and the sooner we teach our children to handle needles and other painful stimuli the better. This can begin from when they are babies with the techniques being modified as they grow up and learn new skills at different stages of development.

144

Resources for parents

* **A Child in Pain** - by Leora Kuttner
(Published H&M 1996).

* **Management of pediatric pain and distress
due to medical procedures** - in MC Roberts
(Ed) *Handbook of Pediatric Psychology.*
NY: Guilford 2003.

* **Sydney Children's Hospital website**
Health Information, *Factsheets on pain and
procedural pain and operations*

* **Annie Stories** *(a special kind of story telling)*
by Doris Brett, Workman NY 1988

Dr Angela Mackenzie
Royal Children's Hospital Melbourne

Conscious Parenting

The idea for this short essay grew out of my observation as a nurse of children and parents in a hospital/medical setting undergoing fearful or painful procedures. *Why do some children cope better?*

The child's innate personality obviously has an impact, but very young children basically reflect their parent's response. This places a responsibility on the parent to be aware of their own behaviours in these settings. I am aware that this can be very challenging and difficult, depending on the parent's own history. I can only encourage you to consider the idea.

I would like to share with you an incident from my own childhood. I was raised by fearful parents. My parents were scared of needles, dentists, doctors, injury, and spiders… the list is endless. Consequently I was a very fearful small child. I can remember watching my mother almost crying when I was having an injection. This continued my belief that whatever was happening was very bad. I became terrified of all medical situations.

When I was about 13 years old, I entered a dentist's surgery crying. The dentist sat me down and asked me why I was crying, I can still remember the room, the dentist and the conversation:

"I'm scared" - *Ellen*
"Of what?" - *Dentist*
"It will hurt" - *Ellen*
"For how long?" - *Dentist*
"I don't know" - *Ellen*
"A week - a month?" - *Dentist*
"No - maybe an hour!" - *Ellen*
"Well - I'll try not to hurt you.
If I do, I am trying to help you and it will be over quickly." - *Dentist*

That conversation had a huge impact on me, he barely said anything, but he was honest and

it taught me even then to examine my fears. We are often scared of events or situations out of proportion to the likely consequences, and this will place undue stress on ourselves and our children.

As parents we constantly make decisions that affect the lives of our children. Even if we don't consciously make an informed decision on a given subject, then the effect is still obvious. I can remember reading about conscious parenting when my children were very young and being aware of the enormity of the statement - everything we do or don't do has an effect! It is out of this consciousness that I began to develop an awareness and understanding of how children respond to stress in the context of illness and injury.

As a basic survival mechanism young children respond to situations according to their parent's behaviour. If the parent is upset or frightened the baby or toddler will become frighted also. It's as a nurse I frequently see children receiving medical treatment. If the parent is calm and matter-of-fact the child copes far better - they may still be upset, but psychologically they are stronger.

I am aware that to ask a person to remain calm in fearful circumstances requires a huge sense of will, but the benefits for the child are enormous. In any situation where a child's life or well-being is threatened through injury or illness, I would encourage parents to consciously choose to develop a sense of strength for the child. Knowledge and honesty are the key to maintaining this sense of strength. Ask questions and gather all of the information you need to honestly support the child. Obviously long complicated explanations are not helpful for young children, a simple honest statement is most appropriate.

For example: "The doctor has to look at your hurt arm so he can help fix it", then calmly holding the child through the procedure is the best approach. Constant requests like "Don't cry, it won't hurt", "be quiet, mummy will buy you a treat" or "stop it now", are not helpful. Crying is okay and it is a child's way of saying all the words they can't use. Lying about it not hurting when it does, destroys the child's trust in the people involved. Panicking and raising your voice only confirms the child's fears that something terrible is happening.

Instead, hold the child firmly and lovingly and say "you have to have a needle now, it will hurt a little, but be over soon". Then it is no longer necessary to beg them not to cry or to say much else, until it is over and you can reassure them. The attitude that you do this with is important. A child will know if you are fearful. Remember also that as a parent how you handle the aftermath of any accident, injury or illness will strongly impact on the child's overall impression and affect how they respond to future situations.

To illustrate this I would like to share a traumatic event that happened to my third son, just after his 6th birthday. I received a call from my husband at work, telling me without explanation to come home. I arrived home to find that my son had been severely bitten on the face by the neighbour's dog, a Rhodesian Ridgeback, after being invited over to pick lemons. He had extensive lacerations and his lips and tongue were no longer fully attached inside his mouth. He looked appalling and I was horrified, however, I had a lot of practice at consciously getting a grip on myself. So I took a deep breath and explained that we had to go to the hospital.

On the way I cuddled him and explained that it was a bad bite and a doctor would need to look at him and decide how to fix it. I also explained that he would ask his doctor friend to look as well, so that they could decide together. As my son progressed through casualty, theatre and ward, I briefly explained each step.

Sometimes as each step occurred he would give me a cheeky look as if to say "I knew that".

As parents, calmly gather information and explain it to the child in simple, non-emotive language. If a child asks a question and you don't know the answer, just say, 'I don't know but I will find out'. Then do it.

We didn't mention the dog or replay the situation for every adult that entered the ward, or in any way make a drama. We certainly de-briefed our friends but not in front of my son. When my son asked a few days later why the dog bit him I told him that I didn't know and it was hard to tell what dogs are thinking, he might have been sick or scared.

My son recovered well after fantastic plastic surgery and never showed any fear of dogs. A few months later we saw a similar dog in the park, I looked at my son wondering if this would be the moment he showed fear. "What kind of dog is that?" he asked the owner. The owner replied "part Rhodesian Ridgeback" and my son's response was "Well, I hope it's not the mouth part!"

I am sure that part of my son's personality allowed him to respond in this fashion, but his strength in knowing that he could cope and therefore he was safe must have contributed. I encourage all parents to consciously examine how they approach illness and injury and encourage them to develop a sense of equanimity; even children with life threatening illness would benefit from a quiet sense of strength.

Ellen Rowatt
Registered Nurse Dip 1,
Grad Dip Women's Health

Index

149

Emotional Conditions

Types of Treatment

Recipes

Vegetable Recipes

GRAIN & PULSE RECIPES

TOFU RECIPES

BEEF & LAMB RECIPES

CHICKEN RECIPES

FISH RECIPES

SALADS

SOUPS

SAUCES & DRESSINGS